Illuminate Your Brilliance with A R C C

(Awareness, Responsibility, Change, Create)

Are Limiting Beliefs Holding You Back?

This book can help you to unleash the brilliance within. Whatever it is you want for your life know that you can create it, with the limitless power of your subconscious mind.

Freedom Series Book 3

Mike England

THIS BOOK IS DEDICATED TO

ALL THE CLIENTS I HAVE HAD THE
PLEASURE TO WORK WITH AND MY
BEST FRIEND LINDA JONES FOR HER
CONTINUED HELP AND SUPPORT.

I WOULD ALSO LIKE TO THANK MY
MOTHER FOR HER CONSTANT LOVE AND
SUPPORT AND ALSO MY WONDERFUL
PARTNER DARREN WITHOUT WHO, NONE
OF THIS WOULD HAVE BEEN POSSIBLE.

CONTENTS

AWARENESS

RESPONSIBILITY

CHANGE

CREATE

CHAPTER 1.

Who Am I

This is my third book in the freedom series and before I start I want to talk a little about me and my life, just to place things into context for the rest of the book. Like a lot of people I have had quite a varied childhood of traumatic experiences and wonderful experiences.

When I was about 10 I remember lying in bed absolutely petrified, all I could think about was death. I kept thinking of the cold dark grave and how I was going to be all alone. The thoughts in my head continued to say to me even if I die with someone in the very same second, we will still be isolated from each other and I would still be alone. *(This stated a lot about my mental state at the time and what beliefs were active, however I did not realise this then).* These thoughts continued to invade my awareness for the rest of the evening and kept me awake most of the night. I asked in my mind in the most powerful way I could, please help me, I need to understand this, show me the answer, someone please show me the answer. I felt quite desperate.

For a kid this was quite a profound experience, I did not realise at the time I was calling upon the power of my subconscious mind by asking for help, which I now know can affect the reality around me and create the experiences of my life.

A few weeks later I noticed a shop I had never seen before, it was called WITCH WAYS, and it was a shop of the occult. They are ten to a penny now, but in the early 1980's, crystals were barely heard of let alone witchcraft shops. I was intrigued and every Saturday would go in the shop and speak to the owner who claimed to be a witch. I would buy books and different paraphernalia with the money I had earned from my paper round.

I purchased and read numerous books on numerology, astrology and other occult subjects,

I also spoke to the owner as much as I could. I began to realise I understood the concepts really easily, anyone who has ever studied astrology or numerology knows how difficult that can be. To me it did not feel like learning, it felt more like I was remembering something I had forgotten.

I wanted to join the witch group, but the owner stated I was far too young and that I would have to wait a few years. This infuriated me as I had a thirst a quest for knowledge, or to put it more bluntly a quest for knowledge of the unknown. At the time I could not understand why no one else I knew was interested in these mysteries.

I did however start meditating at this time, and the owner of the shop helped me to do this. She explained to me that meditation is not about doing, it is more a state of being, it is a space between worlds, a space between thoughts. I was fascinated and so I followed the simple exercises I was given. After weeks of attempting meditation nothing seemed to happen, I explained this to the owner of the shop and she stated to me, "stop trying", I said "what", She said again "stop trying" and then explained you are not looking to achieve anything or go anywhere all you are doing is allowing yourself to experience the space between thoughts. Light bulb moment I suddenly understood, I was trying so hard to make something happen instead of just being, instead of just allowing the experience to happen in the moment free from expectation. *(Another lesson for law of attraction learned, but we will get onto that later.)*

From this moment literally within days things started to change. I began to meditate everyday and still do, within a few days of meditating the right way, I had what I call a life changing experience, I had an out of body experience. I floated out of my body just a few feet and looked back and could see my body. I had no control over this experience and it only lasted a few seconds, but it was one of the most lucid and clear moments of my life. I also began to see things, an example of which my aunt died when I was very young and I used to see her standing in the corner of my bedroom. I would also say things and they would come true. This actually petrified my mother, she even brought a priest to the house, for me it was fascinating, and I wanted so much to explore the true nature of reality, and wanted so much more. These experiences continued for a few years, then when I was 16 I was old enough to join the witch group, so I went back and asked the owner again.

I arrived at the shop and before I even spoke she said yes you can join, but it is in Hednesford. My heart sunk, as this was 15 miles away with limited bus routes and I could not drive, and it was in the evening. I said yes I would love to join the group, and thought (*I will find a way, a way will be shown to me this is what I want and it wIll happen, another lesson in law of attraction.*)

I went on with my day not thinking much about the problem of how to get there, but instead I thought about the excitement of what I would learn, of what it would be like. I was so excited I was ready to burst. Just as the day was ending I had a phone call on the landline. *(Yes people really did use them back then).*

It was the owner of the shop, she stated that two more people had joined the group and they literally lived around the corner from me and she had asked if they would kindly bring me with them each week. I could not contain myself, it was like all of my christmases had come at once. I said my goodbyes and got off the phone to immediately, call them to make arrangements.

Going forward, I learned about meditation, spell casting, talisman making, crystal gazing and numerous other skills. We followed a system called the cabalistic system of high magic, and a few years after that I learned the Wiccan system of magic. I even used to advertise my services in the prediction magazine, and still have testimonials from clients I helped with spells, talismans and healings for specific situations. What was interesting, whenever I did a spell I always asked for the spell to remove the obstacles preventing money, love, or whatever it was from coming into their life. I never asked for the actual thing.

During this time my intuitive powers continued to grow and I had several more out of body experiences, but nothing was like that first one.

I had an intention always in my head throughout all of this period. The intention was to bring all the information I had learned into the public domain free from ritual and dogma. I knew this could be done. I knew the power did not truly reside in rituals or paraphernalia. All those were just tools to focus the tremendous power of the mind. I also knew from the spells and healings, that the mind could truly affect reality. I had seen it for myself. I then started to think about if the mind truly affects reality, how much of reality is affected. This took me on another path completely.

As soon as I asked this question, it was like something opened up inside me. I started to feel more connected to myself and my environment than I had ever been before, goosebumps began to flow through my body. This was a pivotal point for me as it was the start of my new journey of learning to what is now known as the law of attraction, cosmic ordering, manifestation.

It was from this moment in time I used to experience what I now call downloads. In other words I would receive downloads of information, there was no formality involved, I would just be talking to someone who would have a problem and without any foresight I would just know what to say and what to do to help that person. Once

I had given the advice or help it would be like the information was not needed any longer so I would struggle to remember it. I did not know at the time that this is what was happening as it felt so natural.

I have never been materialistic and in fact I only gained employment just to meet my basic needs, why not cast a spell you might say, well the fact is when you cast a spell in order for it to work, you have to release your attachment to it. That is quite easy when you do it for someone else, however when you do it for yourself its not quite so easily done. *(Sounding familiar all of these are law of attraction principles).* I still had not put all the pieces together but I could feel a jigsaw building in my mind.

I eventually got a job in accounts which my parents loved, but I hated, I hated it with a vengeance and did this for nearly 15 years. Then one day I'd had enough.

I said to myself at the computer screen if "I retire and am still doing this, I might as well be dead". This was an incredible moment for me because something stirred within me, a feeling, an urge and incredible energy. Instantly I began looking on the internet for other jobs, and by complete accident I stumbled upon a course in hypnotherapy, I felt so drawn to it and wanted to do it. I was living with my partner at the time Darren and I told him how I felt and he did not judge all he said was if you want to do it, just do it, and he even loaned me the money to do the course. Well this was amazing not only had I found something I felt passionate about, I also had the means to do it.

So I started my training as a hypnotherapist and it was so familiar to me. I recognised a lot of the things I had learned in my witchcraft training were very similar. This allowed the hypnotherapy training to come really easily to me.

Fast forward to now, I realise that a lot of the information I receive intuitively is actually a download from my subconscious mind / creative self/ higher mind, or whatever you wish to call it. I recognise that it contains all the answers, and can literally create whatever you want for your life, in your life.

Hypnotherapy has taught me that by changing someones beliefs, you can literally change a persons life, as I have changed my own using the very same techniques. Just like with the spells of the past I asked for the obstacles to be removed from the persons life, hypnotherapy is similar in the fact that I help remove the beliefs that are holding someone back from what they want.

Through this book I want to help you to do the same. I want you to feel in control of your life, to feel empowered in your life, to create a better life. To be truly connected to yourself and your true nature.

So let's begin.

CHAPTER 2.

Introduction

From all my vast knowledge and experience I have created a system called A.R.R.C:-

- A. Awareness
- B. Responsibility
- C. Change
- D. Create

If you have read my previous two books you will know that I like a simple no nonsense approach to utilising the power of the mind. In my last two books I provided techniques for dealing with beliefs in general. In this book, I will show you how to deal with core beliefs that can really impede your progress to creating the reality you want to live.

All the techniques I present to you I have used on myself and the clients I have worked with on a one to one basis and in the group workshops I have had the pleasure of presenting. This is the reason I write this third book, at the bequest of all the people I have helped utilising this system.

This book is also slightly different as all the techniques for each chapter will be recorded personally by me for you to use. You can gain access to these recordings at this website. www.illuminateyourbrilliance.com

Creating powerful changes in your life, does not require you to be powerful, it does not even require you to have high intelligence. All that is required for you to create powerful changes that can literally transform your life is a slight adjustment of thoughts.

It's strange that we live in a society where we are never taught how to think healthy nurturing thoughts. So many people suffer stress, anxiety and all sorts of problems as a result of poor thinking, for me it would make perfect sense to teach individuals how to think healthy positive thoughts from a young age which could then allow everyone to thrive and flourish. This is a fundamental thing I teach clients when I am working with them on a one to one basis.

In these pages I give details of how you can change your thought patterns and begin to literally create a new life before you

So before we get on to the techniques to help you change your life. Let's explain a little about how it works, so that you have the understanding and foundations to be able to use the techniques effectively, so that you can begin to create whatever it is you want in your life.

I have written in my previous books about the conscious and subconscious mind so I will not go over that in detail but just as a reminder for those who may not have read my previous books.

There are basically two aspects to the way the mind works, actually there are a lot more but for the purposes of this book we only need to be aware of the two aspects I present to you here.

We have the conscious mind and the subconscious mind. What are these two aspects of the mind, well to put it simply they help you to function in life the conscious mind allows you to make everyday choices and decisions about what you want to do in each and every moment, and the subconscious mind is the part of you that deals with everything else your habits, beliefs memories and emotions and all the physiological processes within the body.

In order for you to effectively begin to create change in your life you do need to understand how beliefs work and most importantly how to identify the beliefs that are holding you back and then you can begin to change them. I am going to split this book into sections in relation to the system I have created called:-

A.R.C.C

- A. Awareness
- R. Responsibility
- C. Change
- C. Create

So to begin, let me first explain to you what I mean about awareness

AWARENESS

CHAPTER 3.

Beliefs.

Awareness is fundamentally about you being aware that you create your reality and that every experience and every situation that exists in your life now is there primarily because of some thought or belief system that is active within you.

The situations you experience in your life everyday are highlighting to you the beliefs active in your life and these active beliefs are creating the current reality that you are experiencing.

What are beliefs? A belief is a practiced thought, a thought that you continue to think until it becomes a habit. But is this truly it, well since my first two books I have gained a greater understanding of what a belief is and I am going to share those insights with you today so you can really grasp what a belief is and how it can impact upon your life, most of the time, without you even realising it.

When you are first born into the world you start to make choices, even as young babies. You choose to want to get from A to B so you practice crawling along the floor and eventually learn to crawl and walk. I want you to understand that those choices to move from A to B are practiced by the new born until the thought becomes a belief, when it becomes a belief that you can crawl or walk you can do it.

This effectively is what a habit or belief is. What I want you to understand is that you can not function effectively without beliefs. Another example would be when you learn to ride a bike, at first you have no idea how to use the pedals or get your balance but over a period of time you learn to ride the bike, you have practiced it enough that it actually becomes a belief. Once you believe you can ride the bike through the practised thought and movements of the body you can then ride the bike. Understand that all of your habits are thoughts that have become beliefs.

In fact this is the fundamental principle that thoughts become things. Things would not exist without someone having thought of it first, action of some form is always required to create those thoughts into things, so it can be misleading to think that when someone is carrying out a technique and nothing is coming its because the technique is not working. Any technique is always a three way process you ask and receive ideas, then action is taken.

There are 100's of examples I could give of how beliefs are created you create them all of the time through the things you learn, through the things you hear from yourself by your inner voice and from what you hear from other people in your life. In fact your entire observations of life are creating beliefs which then allow you to perceive and create the world around you through the lens of the beliefs that are created.

If you believed now that you could be successful, abundant, in fact just lucky in life you would find inspiration flowing to you all the time and your actions would take you where positive opportunities exist, you would embrace those opportunities wholeheartedly allowing that reality to exist in your life. You would be optimistic about life and continually looking and finding solutions on the back of any issue or problem that may arise.

However many people do not believe this. Sadly a lot of people today lack self confidence, feel extreme guilt, experience self doubt and are not truly aware of their true worth or potential in life or society as a whole. From this negative place, their reality is then created, and this can appear as a very different reality from the one that they would like to experience.

In the examples just described are beliefs that help you. In other words the beliefs created enhance the experience and enjoyment of life.

We all experience life through the lens of our perceptions, and our perceptions of life will be determined by the beliefs that we have.

There are however other beliefs that can impede you and and hold you back, these are the beliefs that are the subject of this book.

Lets look at a couple of examples of how beliefs affect us more than we realise:-

You want to ask someone on a date

You are out with friends and you see a beautiful person you would like to ask out, you notice the eye contact and the body language seems to indicate that it would be a positive outcome.

Negative belief becomes active

What if the person doesn't like me, what if I've read the signals wrong, what if I am rejected, what would my mates think. So you make a decision not to ask, or you do ask and make a complete mess of it. (a powerful negative emotion is then created (stress, fear etc)

You apply for a new job

You complete the application form get an interview and have all the necessary knowledge and experience, or feel like it's something that you could easily do.

Negative belief becomes active

What if I'm not good enough, I bet there is someone better qualified than me, what if they don't like me. If I'm nervous I could make a shambles of it. (powerful negative emotions are then created (stress, fear etc)

A brilliant idea flows into your mind that you know can be successful and the rewards can be reaped by you and many others. Maybe its a new business or a new invention, and you feel exhilarated by the idea of it.

Negative belief becomes active

What if it fails, what if I get into debt, I bet there is someone out there doing it already, what if it's not good enough, what if I'm not good enough, it's a big risk, can I risk doing this with the potential of losing everything. What if I'm wrong (a powerful negative emotion is then created (stress, fear etc)

The above are just a few examples of how we can have an experience in life that could be extremely positive, but our beliefs hold us back from making a decision. I have experienced this in my own life many times.

Many years ago I was asked to speak in front of 100's of people, and I was so excited and exhilarated for the opportunity and said yes straight away. (Inspired thought / idea).

After the initial excitement had faded and I began to think about the ramifications, I started to doubt myself, what if I stumble over my words, what if I'm not good enough, what if people are not receptive to what I have to say. A whole load of negative beliefs kicked in, which effectively created so much fear and tension in my life I wasn't coping very well. Eventually the day arrived and I had to stop the car 3 times to be physically sick, I even made a wish to have a car accident so as not to attend the event.

Eventually I arrived and did the event and what happened, I made a mess of the introduction stumbling over my words and had to do it again, I had some of the most difficult questions I have ever had in my entire career, which created more anxiety and fear. However No one at the event even recognised I was struggling internally and they all loved the event, but this was not my experience.

So what was happening.

In effect I had created a fantastic opportunity. I had manifested or attracted this experience because this is what I truly wanted, I then received the inspired thoughts to act. My beliefs however were not up to speed with the opportunity this then created my inner voice to tell a narrative that was negative in other words my beliefs needed to change in order for me to flow with the reality that was being created. The reality that I wanted. The reality I had asked for.

I have heard it said many times just feel the fear and do it anyway.

In my personal experience this approach does not work it just creates greater fear and anxiety and in the end this can lead to physical and mental wellbeing issues. I have worked with many people who have felt the fear and done it anyway and the fear never ever goes, all that happens is the stress levels of the individuals increase, and this can lead to physical or mental wellbeing issues.

It is much better to change the belief so that your beliefs can match the reality that you want to create.

What does all this mean, simply put our beliefs primarily create our reality and experiences of life, in order to create a change in your life it requires that you change your beliefs first.

All the choices that you think you make that are free will, are only made because of a belief that you have, so really your ability to make choices based on free will are only as powerful as the beliefs that you hold.

How many times does someone end a relationship then go into another relationship that is similar or worse.

How many times have people had problems in work and they move to a new position or job and the same problems arise. I have experienced this I used to be bullied in every employed job I had and it was always by a woman. It was only when I changed the belief that the bullying stopped and I found employment which was better.

I want you to think about this.

The choices you make exist because of a belief that you have.

When you are attracted to a particular person, why many people say do I always seem to attract the same type of person.

If you have a belief system that states all men/ women are deceitful, or that you are unworthy of love, you will make choices and experience impulses where you feel attracted to those type of persons that can reinforce the belief, which can be a bad or negative relationships or no relationship at all.

Remember your reality will always support the beliefs that are active within you.

A particular career

You may be attracted to a particular career path, or no career path at all, the choices you make in relation to this will be based on a belief that you have.

Any situation even some health conditions are created because of certain beliefs.

Beliefs are powerful things, I've had clients throughout the years who have been asked to give up smoking or alcohol as it is killing them, but even under the threat of death have not been able to give up these things, or if they have, the belief has transferred to something else, an example would be giving up smoking and replacing it with sweets which comes with its own risks.

The only real way to affect change in your life is to begin to change the beliefs which are holding you back. The brilliant thing to know is I have been changing beliefs for myself and the clients I see for years, and now through the exercises presented in this book you too can begin to change your beliefs.

I have described beliefs in great detail here because it is so important that you create awareness of your beliefs, the ones that are holding you back. The ones that require change.

Lets look at some commonly held beliefs :-

I am too fat

I am too thin

I feel ugly no one will want me

I am always ill, I catch everything going

Things never go right for me

I am so unlucky

I am an idiot

I can't do anything right

I am accident prone / clumsy

I am not intelligent enough

I can't afford it

There is a cost of living crisis

Its not fair they have everything I have nothing

No one will love me

My partners always leave me

I'm not good enough
Money is the root of all evil
Money doesn't bring happiness
I don't need money to be happy
Money does not grow on trees
There are no jobs that pay well
My memory is not good
I am forgetful
If you don't work hard you will never achieve anything
I am only attracted to bad boys /Girls

There are so many beliefs I could mention these are just a few for starters. What I want you to actually notice is how silly some of these beliefs sound in the light of reality.

My memory is not good.

Well in reality your brain processes and remembers more information than the most powerful computer in the world. Everyday it makes countless calculations and accesses numerous memories just to help you. Think about everything that needs to be remembered to read or write or drive a car or walk to a particular destination. In reality this belief is not real, but people believe it to be real and when they believe it to be real it starts to become a reality.

There are no jobs that pay well

There are millions of jobs that pay lots of money in fact I have worked in several industries where numerous employees were working for in excess of 50k a year. There are jobs that pay lots of money but if you have beliefs that prevent you from perceiving this you cannot create this, it will be outside the experience of your current reality, which will make this reality of greater abundance outside of your reach.

My partners always leave me

Say this out loud and listen to the words. There are millions if not billions of people in relationships that have lasted many years and are extremely successful and happy. I myself at the time of writing this book have been in a happy relationship for 21 years. If you believe everyone leaves you, then through the lens of your belief you will experience that reality.

Money does not grow on trees.

Well it used too ! More and more it is just a number on a digital screen. Money is just an exchange of value, if you believe that what you have to offer is of great value and you are worthy of it then that great value will return but if you do not recognise or acknowledge the value of what you give whether its of yourself or a product then that value will not return.

Thinking of it another way no one has gone out and destroyed a load of money, in fact there is probably more money in the world today than there was yesterday, its just about the distribution of money, and that distribution will be in accordance with the value and self worth you believe that you are deserving of.

Above are explanations for just a couple of the beliefs mentioned and when you read them it makes sense and intellectually this should be enough to create that change. However as we perceive our experience of life through the lens of our beliefs, it can be very difficult for us to believe something different even when it is right in front of us.

Just think about this most people believe there is a cost of living crisis right now, but you try convincing a millionaire or billionaire of this. You won't because through the lens of their beliefs money is an abundant resource. Intellectually they may accept there is a cost of living crisis, but because of the beliefs they hold, their personal experience of reality will only be one of abundant resources.

Remember reality is experienced through the lens of your current beliefs.

I would like you to begin thinking about the beliefs that could be affecting you and your reality right now!

CHAPTER 4.

Core Beliefs

Up to this point I have been writing about beliefs in general and how they are impacting your life and affecting the choices you are making, this in turn is responsible for creating the reality you are experiencing right now.

There is however, another aspect of beliefs that I would like you to know about so that you have a thorough understanding of how beliefs are affecting your life on a day to day basis. Once you have this understanding along with the exercises later in the book you will be well equipped to change any belief that is holding you back from the reality that you want to create.

What are core beliefs?

When you were very young between the ages of 0 to 6 you were extremely vulnerable and susceptible to the world and people around you. As a child you are reliant on adults to take care of you, and keep you safe and well fed and clothed and warm.

This is an extremely vulnerable time for a child as most of your core beliefs are created during this time and the experiences you have at this time will very much determine what your core beliefs are.

Core beliefs can determine your moral code, your values and how safe and secure you may feel in the world. They are responsible for how you perceive the world and most importantly how you perceive yourself.

There is no right or wrong in core beliefs, however they will greatly affect your perception of the world experienced, most of them are formed from your own thoughts, observations and experiences of the world between the ages of 0 to 6. So if you are called names and abused constantly your core belief could be the world is not a safe place and that adults are not safe.

As an example you may experience a very traumatic upbringing which brings with it thoughts and experiences of feeling unsafe, and not trusting of the adults around you, you may also think to yourself I'm not special, what's wrong with me that they speak to me like that, I don't deserve to be loved. As these thoughts and the associated emotions form within you, and are practised by you enough they become a belief. A core belief which will then affect you and your life until such a time as the core belief is identified and changed.

Your reality primarily will be created from your core beliefs the reason for this is because you will begin to make choices and decisions in life that will allow the core belief to be active, this is what creates the experiences in your life. So if you want to create a better more joyful life it makes sense to identify and change these core beliefs.

Even if you have had the most loving of childhoods you create core beliefs

Lets look at some core beliefs that stop people creating the life they want to live:-

Feeling unsafe (basic needs not met food, water, warmth, clothing, abuse)

Feeling unloved (no hugs, facial contact, shouted at, screamed at)

Poverty(observing living in poverty, constantly hearing of poverty creating a mindset of not enough)

No sense of right or wrong (morals values not developed)

I am no good

I am unlovable

I am not enough

The world is unsafe (sometimes this can be created from being shielded from the world with the best possible intentions)

No good people in the world

I can't trust adults

I am undeserving

I deserve all the bad that is happening

I am worthless

I feel rejected by everyone and everything

I have no value

I am loathed by everyone

This list is by no means extensive but covers a lot of the most commonly held core beliefs and for the purpose of this book should suffice. I will give you an exercise later on to help you identify your core beliefs but for now what I want you to do is to recognise that within you are core beliefs that the majority of your reality is being created from. This is because all of your perceptions of yourself and the world around you will be primarily through the lens of these beliefs.

If you believe the world is unsafe. You may not take a risk on an opportunity that may come your way.

If you feel unloved you may only create relationships where you feel unloved, or even worse are abused further.

If you believe you are unworthy or undeserving your choices may not allow you to succeed, or you may not feel good enough to do something else or ask for that promotion, or even do well at school.

If you believe the world is bad you will shy away from experiencing life fully.

There are core beliefs that are really positive too, imagine if your core beliefs are like the ones below, how do you think your life would be?,

I am safe

I am loved

I am intelligent

I am special and unique

I have a lot to offer

I truly feel loved

I feel happy and joyful

Good things always happen

Things always work out

The world is safe

I can trust the adults in my life to help

The world is full of opportunity

I have incredible self worth

I am valued by everyone.

Just imagine now if you were creating from the above positive core beliefs what different choices would you make ?, What reality would be created by you? It probably would be very different from the one you currently experience.

I cannot emphasise enough that your reality is created by you, but not by the thoughts your thinking but primarily from the beliefs that you hold in your subconscious mind.

This is why a lot of law of attraction and manifestation books do not work! They tell you to imagine this and imagine that or use a specific affirmation then when the technique doesn't work, its because your not trying hard enough your not visualising well enough, you need to give it more time, or my absolute favourite, it won't come because just talking about it not coming is creating that. Worse still it does come, as in my example of the public speaking, and then your core beliefs prevent you from taking the opportunities presented.

Instant creation or manifestation will happen under these conditions.

If you want to create something that is within your current belief system it will happen or you will make choices through inspired action that will allow you to create what it is that you want.

You could just carry out the exercise in the section on create, however if you have negative beliefs to release, it is better to work through all the other exercises in this book first.

If you want to create something that is outside of your belief system, it will not come until you first change the belief, or it will come but you may feel unable to take the opportunity presented, because of fears and anxieties. This is why this book was created to help you to release those limiting beliefs that are holding you back.

Just one more thing if you remember in the first section on beliefs I explained about beliefs in general. These general beliefs are all derived from a core belief

As an example:-

Romance

General Belief

My partners always leave me
I always have bad relationships

They always have affairs
Ill never get anyone
I like bad boys / girls

Core belief

I feel unloved and unsafe
I can't trust the adults in my life

Money

General Belief

Money doesn't grow on trees
Money is hard to get
If you don't work hard you'll achieve nothing
Money is the root of all evil
Feeling insecure that there is not enough money

Core belief

I am worthless
I have no value

These are just examples, and everyones core
beliefs will differ slightly but if you imagine the core

belief as a circle, and the general beliefs span off from them.

It is fairly simple to find the general beliefs, however you have to examine a little bit further to identify the core beliefs.

MONEY

LOVE

I also want to briefly mention the role of emotions.

It is important for you to understand that emotions are not beliefs, If you are experiencing a powerful emotion whether it be negative or positive, recognise THIS IS NOT A BELIEF! An emotion is experienced as a result of a belief, it is not the belief itself.

On that note lets go to the exercise for this section.

CHAPTER 5.

Bubble of Awareness Exercise.

This exercise I have used 1000's of times with many clients including myself, in numerous ways, and in all sorts of situations.

Before I explain the exercise let me explain its purpose.

You should now be fully aware that you are creating your reality in every single moment.

So as you begin to focus on the reality in front of you, it creates further thoughts which then, feed and support the current belief system which is creating more of what you do not want.

Think of it is like this you are on a train of thought going a hundred miles per hour in the wrong direction. What this exercise helps you to do is slow that train down, so that eventually it is moving slowly enough that you can reverse its direction.

What I want you to do is to focus more on the present moment rather than the thoughts and beliefs that are perpetuating the current reality. The present moment is where all your power resides.

Let me explain further if you are creating reality in any one moment, and in those moments you are focused on what's wrong in your life or what's not working, or am moaning and groaning about not having enough, or not having a good relationship or even just feeling low and depressed you begin to create more of this because that is your focus in the present moment. This is the biggest mistake that you can make.

When I trained to be a hypnotherapist I was told by my trainer, that the subconscious mind will always give you more of what you focus upon. So if you are focused on all your problems or the things that are not going well in your life you will then continue to create more problems, more things to moan about. In my previous book ' Miracles Happen with one good thought' I spend a lot of time explaining that in order to begin changing your life, it is important to feel good, that is true but what do I actually mean by feeling good.

My personal belief is there are only two true emotions unconditional love and Joy, when we feel these emotions we feel a complete feeling of trust, a feeling of love, a feeling that everything is just perfect, that nothing is wrong, that everything is fine.

The truth is you have to detach yourself from the reality that you are experiencing right now to begin to create something new and you can do this.

If you can experience the reality around you but not respond to it in the same way you will begin to slow the train of thought down. You can do this by just understanding:-

That everything is fine, everything is being taken care of, everything is sorting itself out, everything is ok, nothing is wrong, these are just stepping stones in the direction you are going, everything is working out as it should, this is just a blip, things are working out in the perfect way for you right now, its fine, you are fine, its just thoughts everything is being taken care of right now, trust in the process, trust its all ok. These things are happening but fundamentally you are fine, you are alive, you are here, its all working out, in this very moment nothing is wrong and all is well.

As you continue to use the above words with the exercise presented in this chapter you will start to feel different. You want to be creating a real feeling that everything is fine, that things are working out and over a period of time sometimes just a few minutes you will begin to feel more stable you will begin to capture the feeling of complete trust.

As you begin to change your focus you will truly begin to believe and think that everything is truly ok and that everything is working out and this is what I want you to feel. If you are creating in every single moment of your life as soon as you change your focus, even just for a moment, that everything truly is fine you then begin to create from your current reality a new reality where everything is truly ok, and in order for things to be ok in your life things have to change. This begins to slow down the train of thought that has been active, the train of thoughts that are creating your current reality. Do not do this this to create change or it will not work, do this to truly be ok and fine and know and trust that everything is working out perfectly.

But my situation has not changed I really am in debt, I really am in a bad relationship, I really am struggling with my weight, I really am living this horrid life, I really am, I really am, I really am….

The above statement has been said to me many many times by nearly every client I have seen. So let's examine this a bit further so you truly do have a thorough understanding of what I want you to do, then I will summarise the technique in a better way. In order to do this I will give a couple of examples of real life stories, of how this actually works one of which is in my last book 'miracles happen with one good thought'

Example 1

A lady came to me who was experiencing stress, she was having problems in her relationship she said she was going to leave her husband because all he did was moan and groan about the news, about work, and more importantly about her, she said nothing I do is right and I am fed up of it. I love him and don't want to leave him but I cannot take anymore. I worked with this wonderful lady to release the beliefs she held then said to her when you next see your husband next no matter what he says to you, no matter how much he moans, just agree with him, she laughed at me, I said please just give it a go you have paid for my service just trust in my advice. She left and said she she would give it a go.

Three days later she phoned me and asked me if I was a witch and had put a spell on her husband. I said no *(if only she knew)*, why? She then said her husband came in last night with a bunch of flowers and a box of chocolates and took her out for a meal. She stated he did not moan once and was in fact really complimentary towards her. I don't understand it. I explained that all that had happened was by agreeing with him she had stopped focusing on the current reality and had actually focused on a feeling of agreeing with him and this allowed her to begin to create something new, it allowed her to to stop the battle, to stop the internal argument inside and create from a place of I agree with you darling, which created in her a feeling of being at peace and trust in the process. As a result of this her current reality shifted to something that she wanted. A reality of peace and trust.

The only way you can truly do this is by detaching yourself from what is going on in your life and begin to create a new perspective that everything is working out.

Example 2

My brother had a massive seizure and was in intensive care in hospital, my mom was so stressed that she could not function, and all my mom did was experience a barage of negative emotions and stress. Very similar to a fight or flight response.

I asked my mom what is happening in this moment right now. She looked at me and said what do you mean. I said are you with my brother right now, she said no, I said so what is happening right now, she said I'm stressed and worried and upset. I said yes you are but in this very moment what is wrong, she said I am worried, I said yes but what is wrong with this moment with me right now. She then said nothing, I said yes thats right. I am not asking you to not care, I'm not asking you to not love him, but right at this moment you are not with him, and you can take no action to help him so what if you were to just think about the love you have for him, what if you just think that he is going to pull through and that everything is ok, that the right doctors are working with him and that everything is working out perfectly.

I said how do you think you would feel if you do this, she said I would probably feel better, I said yes you would and also you would begin to create a reality where everything is ok, where everything is working out perfectly. I said when you are with him or dealing with him in that moment do what you can to help him, but when you are not with him just focus on everything working out, and that everything is ok. This realisation was a big light bulb moment for my mom.

My brother did recover and leave hospital. The point I wanted to make to my mom was her first response was to worry and call everyone and tell them how bad the situation was, her thoughts, her own narrative began to tell her the worst case scenario, which then created fear and anxiety, which would then have created more things in her life where she would worry and be stressed. The simple question what is happening right now in this moment instantly stopped her in her tracks, because she realised that in that moment, nothing was wrong other than her own fearful thoughts which she has complete control of and can change at anytime. What was interesting though was my mom instantly jumped into fearful thoughts.

Everyone in society has a tendency to focus on the problems in life, and worse still they talk to their friends about how bad things are, and even worse go to groups where they talk about how bad things are. You have to understand that you create in this moment so if your focusing on things not working out in your life, if your focused on poverty or lack of love, or a bad relationship or even self sabotaging thoughts you begin to create a reality from that space which mostly is the same. Reality is continually changing but if you focus upon everything that is not working out, or everything that you have not got you are just creating more of the same thing, so you are not recognising that reality changing, because its changing into the same thing.

This exercise can actually help you to begin to change your focus and be more present when those fearful negative thoughts begin to come, and gradually with practice this can change the way you think in those moments, which will ultimately begin to shift your current reality to something better.

This exercise is written in the book for you to use but there is a recorded version created by myself on my website:- www.illuminateyourbrilliance.com

So now to the actual exercise:-

Close your eyes and just take several deep breaths, each time you breathe out just hear the word relax in your mind, continue to do this for several minutes.

It is important to take your time, and allow yourself to feel each breathe which will allow you to slip into a really calm and peaceful space.

After awhile you may find your thoughts becoming calmer and stiller, when this happens allow your breathe to return to normal and allow yourself to just feel the feeling of tranquility and calm. There is no right or wrong everyone will experience this in their own unique way.

It is important to take your time, there is no need to rush, everything is perfect right now, you are perfect and this moment is perfect.

I want you now to imagine that you are in a nice safe space, a field of beautiful coloured flowers, a beach or just a space inside your own mind.

Take some time to allow yourself to see all the images and feel all the emotions in this safe place. I want you to engage all your senses into this experience.

Now imagine a large glass dome comes down from above you and surrounds your body, it is expansive and clear so you can see through it and it moves with you so is always spacious and airy.

It feels safe and peaceful in here, you feel protected, and clear minded. You feel totally aware of the stillness and peace that envelopes you right now.

This is a perfect place, a place of safety, a place where nothing can touch you, just experience a feeling of complete and total trust.

Now I want you to think about what would it be like right now if the problem did not exist any longer. What if a solution had been found.

What would you be feeling?
How would you be acting?
What would you be thinking about?

What would your conversations be like with others

(In fact imagine having a conversation with a friend or family member where you are telling them that a solution has been found and everything is ok now).

It is important not to imagine anything in particular, What I want you to do is allow the feeling of the problem NOT being in your life right now.

Continue to have the conversation in your mind that everything is sorted and has been taken care of. It is all working out now and everything is fine. It was just a blip, a stepping stone to where you wanted to be. It is all ok now.

Continue in your imagination to have these conversations until you feel soothed, until you slip into a place of complete peace and total trust that everything is truly ok.

When you truly feel this you will know, you will feel that feeling of trust that all is well.

Now I want you to see the things that were bothering you the bills piling up, the bad relationship, the stressful thoughts, the negative situations and the negative people in your life. See them outside of your bubble of awareness.

As you observe the situations and people from inside your bubble notice that they cannot penetrate your shield notice that they just linger outside your bubble trying to get in, but they cannot gain access.

Now increase your feelings of trust and calm, all is well, recognise that you are perfectly safe basking in your feelings that everything ok, that nothing is wrong, that everything is working out, that the problem does not exist in here, solutions exist in here. Everything is working out right now, all is well right now.

Really allow yourself to feel that all is well and that you are at peace. Remain like this for a few minutes.

Now in your mind repeat these words slowly and with feeling in your mind, Calm.......... Peace.......... Trust..........Its all ok, everything is fine.

Do this several times increasing the feelings of trust and peace even further.

Then after a few minutes count yourself awake by counting from 1 to 5 and on 5 state to yourself I will awake refreshed peaceful and calm.

Now begin to count 1,2,3,4,5, open your eyes refreshed calm and peaceful

Now as you go through the day ask yourself frequently

What is happening right now in this moment ?

If there is nothing wrong in your reality and it is just your thoughts about your current reality just think of your bubble of awareness and in your mind repeat the words CALM, PEACE TRUST, ITS ALL OK, EVERYTHING IS FINE, and allow yourself to recapture the feeling that all is well that everything is ok and its all working out for you and that everything is fine.

You can carry out the above exercise as many times as you want, but after a few times or even the first time of using it, you should be able to recapture the feeling that everything is ok when you use the words Calm, Peace, Trust, It's all ok, Everything is fine. What you will have effectively done is create an anchor.

An anchor is where you attach a feeling an emotion to certain words or actions. An example of an anchor would be hearing a song on the radio and instantly being transported to the memory and feelings of a particular situation whether it be a wedding day or holiday.

Now when you are with people that are moaning and groaning about their situation in your mind be with your bubble of awareness and use the words CALM, PEACE, TRUST, IT'S ALL OK, EVERYTHING IS FINE. You can hear what people are saying but you are free from the effect of their words there words just move into your awareness and just as easily move out of your awareness.

Anytime you find yourself getting drawn into the current reality, just ask yourself the question, What is happening right now in this moment?, if it is just your thoughts about a situation instantly focus on this bubble of awareness and those words and know that everything is fine, all is well, its working out perfectly.

It is important to do this as much as you can throughout the day, the more you do this the quicker changes will happen.

In just a few days you will begin to see the effects of this exercises in your life. You will begin to trust more that everything is being taken care of, things may even begin to change in your reality. I can't make you do this, however if you follow the exercise faithfully you will begin to feel differently about the situations and people that used to bother you.

This is the first part in the ARCC system and I would advise that you do this exercise for at least a week but preferably two or three weeks before you go onto any of the other exercises.

One more thing before I go onto the next section, I am not asking you to not deal with situations, by all means pay the bills, deal with the problems that come, but deal with them in that moment. As soon as you have dealt with the person or situation take your focus back to trust and the bubble of awareness bask in the knowledge that everything is fine in the moment and nothing is wrong and that everything is being sorted and is working out. The more you do this the easier it becomes to focus on the feeling that everything is fine and everything is working out.

The reason this works is it creates a different mindset within you, a mindset that you can trust that all is well, that everything is ok, that everything is fine. You then begin to create from these thoughts and in order for things to be ok and fine, the problem has to cease to exist.

You cannot pretend to do this because it will not work.

This is something you have to truly feel. You don't do this to change your reality, you do this just to encompass the feeling that everything truly is fine and everything truly is calm and that you truly can trust that it's all working out.

Most peoples thoughts are like this:-

Negative feelings and beliefs from the past (focus on bad things that happened / negative beliefs)

Negative feeling and thoughts in the present (focus on the worst of current reality,)

Pessimistic about the future (worst case scenarios)

The optimum way to be, which can happen if you follow the steps in this book is:-

Release the beliefs from the past.
Feel and focus good thoughts in the now
Be optimistic and expectant of good things in the future. (plan for everything to always work out)

Remember when you are in the midst of a crisis deal with it, take action, you have to it is your only option. However most people are not in the midst of a crisis all the time, instead they are in the midst of their own thought patterns, their own beliefs. Which create powerful negative emotions. This is what I am asking you to change with the bubble of awareness. So please commit to yourself and give it a go. It literally can change your life.

Example 3

I had a call from school to say that one of my children was truanting I instantly went into panic mode where are they, what's happening, I need to find them all the fearful type thoughts, then I remembered what I advise clients. In the very moment I had the call I was on the motorway and could not do anything other than think and drive. I couldn't deal with the situation directly so what I did was focus on the bubble of awareness, everything is fine, it's all ok, its all working out, its all being sorted. I did this and it soothed me and I slipped into a place of complete trust that everything was fine in that moment. My child was still missing but in that moment I had a choice to experience fearful thoughts or soothing thoughts, I could not physically take any action in that moment. When I got off the motorway I had another call from the school to state that my child had returned to school and everything was fine.

Most people worry about things constantly, I am asking you to deal with situations when you physically can such as when the bill needs paying, or when you are with the person you are concerned about, but if the bill doesn't need paying until Friday, or your not seeing the person until the next day don't waste your creation power thinking fearful thoughts, think about the bubble of awareness and slip into trust that all is well, and just see what happens. Until you do this, you will never know how powerful it is.

If I had continued to focus in the fearful / stressful way I would have created more of that in my life. However I didn't, I knew in that particular moment I could take no action, other than changing my own thoughts so this is what I did and then the reality changed to match that. Most of the time the stress and fear that people think is because they are constantly regurgitating the same negative thoughts from the negative experiences in their lives moment to moment day by day. Change this now and watch your life begin to transform.

If you are in a job you hate, don't constantly think I hate this job, think the thoughts of your bubble of awareness and allow yourself to slip into trust. Then you will begin to create something different.

I used this in a very unique way over 12 years ago when I wanted to leave the accountancy job I was in at the time. I was using the bubble, but back then I called it the bubble of protection, and I knew I created from the present but hated my job so much I could not find anything to enjoy, so I got really creative in my mind when I was in the office.

I started saying to the office equipment, goodbye phone thank you for looking after me and providing for me but it is time for me to go now, I am now ready to move onto pastures new. I used to make statements like this in my mind constantly throughout the day, and even when I left to go out at night I used to say goodbye building thank you for looking after me and taking care of me but its time to go now I am ready to move on. I even used to imagine the building waving at me and saying goodbye.

It sounds silly but after a few days I really started to feel soothed by the words I felt really comfortable and calm, I had a feeling that everything was going to be fine. At that time I had also set up my hypnotherapy business which was still building so I was not in a position to give up a full time job, I had fears what if it does not work, what if I don't earn enough etc etc etc.

I continued with the exercise, the first thing that happened was after a week I started getting more client appointments in fact they had doubled, but I still did not feel comfortable enough to leave the 9 to 5 job, then a week later I had about 15 clients book which was astounding !! I just thought in my head ok I'm getting the message, then one morning I had this incredible urge *(inspired thought)* to just hand my notice in, the urge was so powerful it just took over me, and that is exactly what I did, I handed my notice in and from that moment I had a constant flow of clients, not just clients, but other opportunities started flowing into my life too. All from using the above exercise.

I am not by any means stating that bad things don't happen, they do, what I am asking you to do is only focus on those bad things when you need to make a decision or to take some form of action. All the other times focus on the bubble of awareness and in time you will begin to find that bad situations happen less and less, or solutions come almost as quickly as the problems.

CHAPTER 6.

Summary of Exercises

Carry out the bubble of awareness exercise as described in the previous chapter, or listen to it here www.illuminateyourbrilliance.com

Ask yourself the question frequently through the day

What is happening right now in this moment?

If you find it is just your thoughts about a situation or person and you are not physically experiencing the actual situation begin to think of the words CALM, PEACE, TRUST, IT'S ALL OK, EVERYTHING IS FINE. Speak the words in your mind like a lullaby and allow yourself to be in the bubble of awareness which will then allow you to slip into a place of trust and peace that all is well, and that everything is working out.

Remain in this place of trust and peace as long as you possibly can and allow it soothe you.

Now we will move onto the next section responsibility.

RESPONSIBILITY

Chapter 7.

Take Responsibility

This chapter can be a bit of a difficult pill to swallow for a lot of people, myself included, but it is really important for you to understand this. Without this fundamental understanding you will not be able to identify and change the beliefs that are holding you back.

In order for you to begin creating a new reality, you have to take responsibility for the reality you are already experiencing. You have to recognise through awareness that you are creating every single moment of your reality, the angry neighbour next door, the leaking tap in the kitchen, the wonderful holidays in fact every single thing in your life is created by you and in order for you to move forward you have to take responsibility for this.

Understand and recognise more than anything else, that anytime you moan and groan about a particular person or situation in your life that is causing you grief or upset you are disempowering yourself,

Really think about this every time you moan and groan about a person or situation you are truly disempowering yourself.

Why I hear you say? Well as I have explained in the previous chapter you are currently making choices and decisions based on your core belief system which creates the current reality you are experiencing. If your core beliefs are negative you will create situations to experience this, because your current beliefs want to survive and thrive in your life, and as these situations are then created, and you then blame outside circumstances or other people you actually disempower yourself.

You cannot state in one breathe I create my reality, then in another he did this to me, or she did that or work are placing too much pressure on me. That is not taking responsibility, taking responsibility is asking questions such as:-

What do I want to create in my life right now?

I wonder why I created this reality? *(what do you believe about this reality).*

What do you feel about the current reality (your name)?

What is all this about (your name)?

What is the core belief preventing me from changing my current reality?

For a lot of people this is a lot to take in because it means taking responsibility for every single person, every single situation, and every circumstance you experience in life. We are accustomed in our lives to completely disempowering ourselves. We have, as a society made an art form of moaning and groaning by means of news channels, dramas on TV, social media, moaning about our health conditions and even in our social circles moaning about the people in our lives and usually the ones we are meant to love the most.

These are all survival tactics of the belief system that is active within you, beliefs wants to survive, they want to thrive and when you are not taking responsibility for every single thing in your life you are empowering the limiting beliefs to create more of the current reality.

When you start to ask and ponder the questions above you begin to question the belief. This actually stops the practiced thought in its track for that moment, allowing you the opportunity to examine the belief further and find the core belief that is active within your life. When you play the blame game there is no opportunity whatsoever to identify any belief let alone a core belief that could literally change your life.

A lot of people can struggle with beliefs that are active as there is usually a powerful emotion associated with them whether it be fear, anger, sadness, stress, helplessness and many others I could mention.

I want you to understand more than anything else that the emotion is only experienced as a result of the belief that is active, in particular the core beliefs.

Think of the emotions as trying to prevent you from looking any further into your beliefs. When you feel the emotion you either start the blame game out there in life, or even worse the blame game within yourself which creates a feeling of powerlessness.

Just know that these emotions are a result of a core belief that is active within you, and recognise that the core belief within you that is creating the emotion is also creating the situations you are experiencing in life. This creates an awareness that you truly do have the keys within you to begin creating a better reality. The reality you want to live. You begin to take responsibility and recognise how POWERFUL YOU TRULY ARE !

We experience a range of emotions in life, excitement, enthusiasm sadness, anger, hate, love with conditions, and a lot of these emotions create an adrenaline or chemical rush within us. Now science recognises that adrenalin is good for us initially, however over a prolonged period of time it can create damage in the body. This is why stress can be so dangerous it releases adrenalin which was originally for our flight or fight response.

It is not just negative emotions that release adrenalin, emotions such as excitement and enthusiasm release adrenalin too.

There is no difference physiologically between the emotions of fear and excitement other than the thought behind the emotion. Physiologically the body carries out the same mechanism.

My personal belief is that there are only two emotions that truly exist and they are Love and Joy, all the other emotions experienced are in one form or another supporting or protecting a belief system within you and therefore are secondary emotions.

When I talk about love I do not mean the love with conditions placed upon it. I mean the unconditional love that a mother has for a child or a child for a mother. This type of emotion is very different it feels different. It does not feel like the ocean fluctuating from one thing to another.

Unconditional love is just a constant that exists whether you focus on it or not. This is the best place to be in because it creates a feeling of complete and total trust. This is what creates a positive happy reality. For many people in order to create from this place, core beliefs have to be changed. We can however, use as I like to call them, the secondary emotions to help us identify the general and core beliefs and that is the subject of the next chapter.

CHAPTER 8

How to Recognise Beliefs.

How do we recognise the beliefs that are holding us back. Well it is quite simple really, you just have to look at the life you are living.

Life is like a great big mirror, in fact it is better than a mirror because the life experiences you are living are an exact replica of the beliefs that you are holding.

So if something is not working out in your life and you begin to feel a powerful emotion in your body such as anger, rage or any number of negative emotions, just acknowledge and accept that the emotion is there and it exists and allow yourself to feel it, but also accept it is within your power to create change now and the powerful emotions you are experiencing are a fantastic opportunity for you to create something new then all you have to do is look at your life and ask yourself:-

What do I want to create in my life right now?

I wonder why I created this reality? *(what do you believe about this reality).*

What do you feel about the current reality (your name)?

What is all this about (your name)?

What is the core belief preventing me from changing my current reality?

If we create our reality from our current beliefs, and our current beliefs utilise emotions to keep us within our existing belief system, by not confronting our emotions and taking responsibility for them we are only creating more of what we don't want. If you truly want to be powerful in your own right and create the reality you want the first step is to acknowledge the emotions you are feeling, as you do this you can then begin to ask the questions above.

When we suppress our emotions or refuse to acknowledge their existence we effectively become powerless and become like a leaf in the wind being blown about everywhere according to our core beliefs. This is not creating your reality. This is creating by default. So begin today to take control of your life.

In order for this to work, I suggest you only deal with one thing at a time, so begin right now to ask yourself what do I want to create in my life?

More money / or specific amount of money
A better job
A promotion
Setting up your own business
An idea to create a constant flow of abundance in your life
Improving your relationship
Creating a new relationship
Improving a health condition
Reducing the fat around your body
Creating greater mental or physical wellbeing

To find out what you actually do want in life
Public speaking
A new home
A holiday

What do you want to create in your life really allow yourself to think about this……

Now you have identified what you want you can begin to ask the questions to identify the beliefs that are active in your life.

In order to do this I will use a couple of examples from my own life using the questions previously mentioned so you can get a clear understanding of how to do this. Then I will summarise the technique at the end of the chapter.

My first example will be the one I used earlier

Not being able to speak in public was holding me back in my career, and after my first experience I did not want to do it again. This situation was preventing me from expanding and helping many more people than I could ever possibly help on a one to one basis, I was offered incredible amounts of money to speak and refused every single one. *(I was actually offered thousands and thousands of pounds and refused to present because this belief was so powerful within me it created fear and anxiety, can you see how beliefs can stop you creating the reality you want).*

Example 1

Public Speaking

The first thing I did was to use the questions below to find out more about the public speaking issue.

So I got a pen and paper and asked the questions below:-

What do I want to create in my life right now?

Answer

I want to create a situation where I am sharing what I know to a larger audience, calmly, confidently and effortlessly.

I wonder why I created this situation? *(What beliefs do you have about this situation)*

So with this second question I am completely and totally bringing my awareness to exactly what I am currently creating for myself, in other words taking responsibility.

Answer

I am in a position where I have been offered an incredible opportunity but because of fear and anxiety I cannot move forward, ultimately that means

I cannot expand my business.
I am powerless.
Maybe I should I give up.
Maybe I Should not even be doing this anymore if I cannot sort this issue out myself.
I've helped others sort this out but cannot help myself.
How do I get past this fear.
What if I never get past this fear.

Now this is where we can use our emotions to explore the beliefs more deeply.

What do you feel about the current reality (Your name)?

Answer

This question started me thinking about how I truly felt about the current situation even more deeply. I have listed them below:-

I felt scared and fearful
I felt anxious and nervous.
In fact I was so scared I would even avoid talking about it to anyone
I could not even accept within myself how great the fear was this in turn created an extreme feeling of powerlessness.
I did not realise at the time that this suppression of my emotions was the negative beliefs greatest power over me.

Previous to this question I used to not even accept that I was feeling this, I use to make stories up or hide away from the emotions pretending they did not exist. I believed that embracing the emotions made me powerless. How wrong was I.

When I asked this question the first thing that happened was I allowed myself to feel the emotions I acknowledged and accepted them and then I wrote them down and continued to ask the next question.

What's all this fear about (your name)? *(Using your own name is an extremely powerful way of asking questions of yourself).*

Answer

After I had experienced the emotion a lot of thoughts / beliefs began to come into my mind about what the fear was, this allowed me to access even more deeply held beliefs about the situation. Notice all my focus was in the future outcome of what may or may not happen.

What if I'm not good enough
What if it doesn't work out
What if I look foolish
What if I forget what to say

What if I am asked something I cannot answer
What if people walk out
What if they boo me out

The reason my beliefs did this is because I truly believed I was a good therapist and really good at what I do so it could not contradict that so instead my subconscious mind had to be creative in telling some fictional story about my future in order to survive. It worked and we all do this all of the time and our creative self will use the past, present and the future to argue why the current belief system needs to remain active within you.

Remember

Negative feelings and thoughts from the past (focus on bad things that happened / negative beliefs)
Negative feelings and thoughts in the present (focus on the worst of current reality,)
Pessimistic about the future (worst case scenarios)

The subconscious mind uses this all of the time to maintain belief systems.

All these statements I recognised were not actually real, the statements were actually fear of something in the future that may or may not happen. I was being pessimistic about the future fearing the worst. So the reality I was creating did not even exist. In actual fact my fears and anxieties about what may happen or may not happen were holding me back from seeing and embracing the opportunities that existed right in front of me in the present. In fact I kept focusing on lottery wins and windfalls of money, which really was an avoidance tactic of the subconscious mind. True creation is not about winning what you want, yet sometimes this happens, true creation is about receiving the inspiration to act in a way so that you create your reality before you.

If you remember before I said that we create from the now moment and if our now moment is full of fear and anxiety, then you begin to create more of it, and that is exactly what was happening for me. I was creating opportunities, but my constant fear and anxiety about the future was stopping me creating a new reality in the present, or more precisely was creating more opportunities for me to refuse.

These statements were my general beliefs and for me they were true and I believed them to be true. So my beliefs created these powerful emotions to ensure that the beliefs were active in my life which would then prevent me from taking the opportunities that were presented to me at that time.

Sadly for many years prior to me carrying out this process, these beliefs did prevent me from carrying out many workshops and talks. Which created an empty feeling inside me because I felt inside that if I cannot thrive doing what I love, what is the point of anything.

Through this process, I created powerful changes and this created a new reality for myself. It did not happen all at once I did it one situation at a time.

The strange thing was, I had been doing this instinctively for many years and I had also been doing this with all the numerous clients who came to see me.

So the answers were in front of me all the time, but the beliefs which created the constant fear and anxiety were preventing me from seeing that the answers to my questions already existed in my reality, through life experience and all the clients I have had the privilege to work with.

The truth is I actually love my work and prior to me even being offered the talks \ workshops I used to daydream about doing them and it felt exciting and fulfilling that I could help so many people to change their lives for the better. When the opportunity arrived the belief wanted to survive so activated powerful emotions within me to prevent me from doing the thing that I love to do which is to help as many people as possible to create better lives for themselves.

This was not the end of the process though, I still needed to identify the core beliefs so I took the general beliefs and began to read them through and really pin them down.

I now asked

What is the core belief preventing me changing my current reality?

Answer

I then knew that all my pessimism relating to public speaking had obviously been triggered by something in my past.

So I looked at the beliefs below to identify the core beliefs that I described earlier and began to realise there was a common theme. This was really interesting for me because I do this instinctively for clients.

Every single belief was stating that I was concerned and worried about what people think, or that I might get something wrong.

What if it doesn't work out
What if I look foolish
What if I forget what to say
What if I am asked something I cannot answer.
What if people walk out
What if they boo me out
What If I am wrong

Instantly this was a light bulb moment and I realised in a flash;

I Did not feel safe with adults
I Did not believe the world was safe

All the connections just fell into place.

This was a revelation for me because I instantly recognised this was because I felt unsafe with adults in general and unsafe in the world, which actually I realise now was created in my younger years, Voila !!! I had identified the core beliefs activating all those fears, anxieties and insecurities. It felt like instant relief. My clients have described this feeling to me and I never truly understood this power until that moment.

Please don't misunderstand me nearly everyone I know and meet think I am the most optimistic, positive person they know, but with this particular issue which most importantly I kept secret and hidden I was not. No one ever knew the true extent of the fears within me at that time.

Example 2

Relationships

What do I want to create in my life right now?

I want to create a committed loving, long lasting relationship, where we both have mutual respect for each other?

The current reality for me in the past was being in emotionally and sometimes physically abusive relationships.

I wonder why I created this current reality?
(What do you believe about the current reality)

Answer

I previously had two relationships, the first one was emotionally and physically abusive. The second one my partner was detached and non emotional and eventually abandoned me without even letting me know. Two very different relationships it seems

I believed I could not do any better
I believed if this relationship ended I would be on my own forever
I believed I could not cope on my own
I believed this relationship was better than no relationship
I was scared of being on my own
I believed that any relationship is better than no relationship
I believed it was not that bad there are worse relationships out there
I believed maybe it was something I had done, and that I should try harder.

This was very interesting at that time, notice there are no what if statements here. The statements are all in the past, my subconscious mind did not have to invent a story from the past in order for me to believe it in the present.

What was more interesting at this time I used to dye my hair pink, blue, black, blonde. I would wear bright coloured clothing to be seen, in fact I would do extremely outrageous things, such as dance in a supermarket for no reason the belief created these impulses, desires and situations so that I would be judged by people, so that strangers would have an opinion of me. *(See beliefs above)* I could've chosen to blend into the crowd but I didn't because the beliefs I had needed to create a reality for me and that reality was of me not liking myself and worrying about what people think.

What do you feel about the current reality Michael?

Answer

I felt helpless.
I felt a victim.
I felt I deserved all the bad things that were happening, I even blamed it on karma for something I may have done.
I felt alone and unsafe.
I felt angry and scared.
I felt constantly anxious waiting for the next round of abuse.
I felt insecure and worried they would leave me.
I felt trapped and could not find a way out.
I felt death would be a blessed relief because the anguish would then stop.

I then asked?

What's all this about Michael?

Answer

On examining my emotions I began to notice more deeply held beliefs that were present.

I didn't like who I was
I believed I deserved all the abuse
I could not be myself
I believed I was not attractive
What would anyone see in me
I bet everyone pretends to like me
I would see someone in the street and think of all the bad opinions they have of me
I even believed people were just pretending to be my friends

What is the core belief preventing me from changing my current reality?

Answer

When I asked this question and looked at the responses to the other questions I had answered I recognised in an instant that this was more about my relationship with myself and not my relationship with a partner. I then started to think about the beliefs I had with myself or more importantly the beliefs I had about the relationship with myself.

As I did this a common theme emerged all the beliefs that I had back then were about me not feeling any self worth. I did not actually like who I was. In that instant I knew what the core belief was. I thought originally it was about self esteem but in actual fact it was about self worth.

I felt unworthy of myself and unworthy of being loved.

This time my subconscious mind created these beliefs from the past because for me, I truly believed them.

Negative feelings and thoughts from the past (focus on bad things that happened / negative beliefs)

Negative feelings and thoughts in the present (focus on the worst of current reality,)

Pessimistic about the future (worst case scenarios)

You will be pleased to know that I shifted that belief very quickly and my reality changed almost as quickly and I am now in a really good loving relationship and have been for over 20 years.

Example 3

Money

Until about the last 20 years I always struggled with money and more importantly holding onto money. My reality was one of work hard, earn money, pay bills. It is like this for a lot of people. It always felt like a great weight on my shoulders it did not matter how much money I earned, the money would go just as quickly whether it was me overspending or unexpected bills and expenses. At one point I had three jobs just to make ends meet. This still was not enough and I ended up homeless and then luckily a kind friend let me stay in their room for awhile until I got myself back on my feet. This was my reality for many years.

I did all the techniques other books state cosmic ordering, imagine this, imagine that. Nothing worked but truth be known at that time I could not even believe my imagination could create a different reality. I was so weighed down by my beliefs of poverty and this was creating more poverty in my life. Everything I was experiencing back then was just too big in my reality for me to even see a way through. How did I change this?

What do I want to create in my life right now?

Answer

I want to create a situation where there is a constant flow of abundance in my life to do all the things that I want to do

I wonder why I created this reality? *(what do you believe about this reality).*

Answer

I knew I was creating my reality so one day I put the books away and asked myself seriously, what is the reason you are creating this. There is some message in the poverty, I wonder what it is, there is some reason, some belief, some thought pattern that needs to change. Just speaking like this got me thinking in a different way. It made me feel like maybe just maybe there was something I could do. So I began to write down what I believed about money the list I created is below:-

Money is hard to get.
It does not grow on trees.
There are more poor people than rich people.
How can I get money, I cannot even see a way forward.
If I don't work hard il'l never get anything in life.
If I have not got a good qualification I will never succeed.
(And the worst belief of all)
If I don't have money I cannot be happy.

Maybe because I feel insecure I'm creating insecurity.

Life is meant to be a struggle.

Now I want you to be aware of a big contradiction I had three jobs and was working really hard, and also I had good qualifications. Even though I worked hard and had qualifications I did not have large amounts of money. This is just an example to show you how our subconscious mind continues to make up stories for us to believe to keep the core beliefs active.

What do you feel about the current reality (your name)?

Answer

When I asked this question it opened up a whole world of emotion that I had avoided thinking or feeling about. Remember to acknowledge and accept, you're emotions this is the way to get to the core beliefs. Also notice my wording all of these beliefs were related to the past in some way. My subconscious mind was again using my past to create my current reality.

I felt out of control

I felt overwhelmed

I felt like giving up

I felt like I had nothing to offer anyone

I felt like I was not special or unique

I felt I had no skill set to create money

I felt angry

I felt sad

I felt depressed. *(in fact I sat down and cried my eyes up)*

I felt so totally powerless

I felt their was no way out and what was the point of living

I felt underserving of nice things, I could not even comprehend receiving them

What's all this about Michael?

Answer

I asked this question and looked at how I felt about the current reality. I began to recognise that I was giving up on myself, I believed I had nothing to offer anyone, or if I did offer myself or skills that they were nothing special. I believed that someone else could probably do what I was doing ten times better than me.

If I thought these things why shouldn't everyone else believe it too.

I then went onto the next question

What is the core belief preventing me from changing my current reality?

Answer

I read the answers to the questions over and over and then checked the core beliefs list and there it was, it just stood out in front of me.

I believed I had no value
I believed what I had to offer had no value

Once I realised this I carried out the process of change which is in the next chapter and instantly I began to notice a change in money. Money started arriving in my life. Debts I was owed were suddenly paid. I suddenly started having an influx of more and more clients. Before long I actually had savings in the bank, I could buy nice things. My mortgage was paid, the cars were paid for I started to see opportunities all around me, and yes I even won money. All of this happened just by changing the core beliefs above. Now I am fortunate enough to be in a position where money just flows in easily and constantly.

Example 4

Body Image / Shape / Size

All my life I had issues about my body size, even when I was younger and was extremely thin, I used to believe I was too fat. This carried on long into my adult life and created much misery in my life. It got to the point where I did put weight on because I had told myself so many times I was fat I eventually believed it and put 3 stone of fat onto my body without even realising. I tried diets, these worked in the short term but I never was truly happy restricting myself, I always believed deep down there must be a better way I went to the gym and still do in fact I found from this I love doing the classes.

Nothing seemed to work for me, this caused me to think about my shape even more, yet frustratingly at the time I was working with a lot of clients who were obese and they were successfully shifting the fat and changing the shapes of their bodies. *(Remember life reflects what you most need to learn / change)*. So I used the techniques in this book to create a change in my reality about my body shape.

What do I want to create in my life right now?

I want to create a slim slender body, a body I feel comfortable and happy with.

I wonder why I created this reality? *(what do you believe about this reality).*

Answer

I really started to think about this question. What on earth would I want to create this situation for. I knew I did not want to be overweight but I also knew that I had created this. I just allowed my awareness of the situation to really sink in, I struggled with this one so I just began to think about my actual body I did not like it, I did not feel comfortable in my own skin.

This question brought a whole plethora of information to the surface. See the list below:-

I believed my body shape was too big (even when it was thin)
I believed I couldn't change anything
I believed I looked disgusting and it made me feel sick
I believed what would anyone else see in me when I don't like the fat
I believed it was beyond my control to change it because food was everywhere it could not be avoided
I believed that eating would make me feel better
I believed if I ate in secret no one would know
I believed I was not in control
I believed I was big boned and there was nothing I could do
I believed it was genetic (yes at one point I believed this and even had a genetic test)

I believed if I could control and restrict my food intake it would work

I believed people would make a judgement because of the fat

I believed my body was fighting me every step of the way and making it hard

I believed my body was the enemy

I believed food was the enemy

Do you see how many beliefs I had about my body shape when I actually began to write them down. There were so many, and these beliefs were constantly active in my life every time I was around food, every time I ate food, every time I went shopping. I could not actually avoid them. I did use the bubble of awareness and this is what allowed me eventually to begin to see things in a different way, it created a gap so to speak in my thinking about my body.

What do you feel about this situation Michael?

Answer

I felt disgusted in myself

I felt anguish

I felt uncomfortable in my own skin

I felt like I was constantly self sabotaging myself

I felt powerless and overwhelmed

I felt unhappy

I felt really really angry with myself

I hated myself

I felt depressed and low

I felt like I did not want to go out in the world

I felt like I needed to hide away after all I was disgusted in this so everyone else would be

I felt out of control and helpless, not knowing what to do

I hated who I was

I felt a complete failure

When I read through the list I was literally quite shocked at how I truly felt. I did not realise the extent of how I felt until I wrote it down. I actually began to cry. I knew I was not a bad person, but I felt all those things towards myself. My gran was overweight and I did not feel those things about her I just loved her, so what was the reason I was feeling these things about myself. I want you to also notice I use the word I felt, I believed, this was a big indicator that it was something way back in the past that was affecting my present and ultimately my future. I just want you to notice that the subconscious mind used a lot of tactics in order to keep the current beliefs active. I knew I was a good person, I knew I was kind, I knew I was confident, I knew I had empathy and compassion. So in order for that belief to become active, my subconscious mind had to sift through my past to create a situation where I would be confronted with these negative beliefs so that I could deal with them.

What's all this about Michael?

Answer

As I read through the list I suddenly realised that every single one of the answers was all about self loathing, and not being comfortable with me or who I was, they were all about me not loving or even liking myself. All the beliefs active were about that deep sense of belonging and nurture that we all crave.

I then asked the next question

What is the core belief preventing me from changing my current reality?

Answer

I read everything I had written down and suddenly I knew what the core beliefs were, they just stood out as I read through the list of negative core beliefs I could feel the activation of the beliefs within me. I have listed them below:-

I believed I was not enough for me or anyone
I believed I was unlovable
I believed I was was loathed by everyone including myself

This realisation was so big and massive within me. I felt like something that had been hiding from me all of my life had suddenly had a massive beam of light shone upon it.

I am not stating that you always have to find a core belief. I have worked with many clients who have experienced many things in their lives that have sometimes come from trauma as an adult. My other books attest to this and the techniques in both those books have worked very successfully for a lot of clients, to change general beliefs.

What I am stating is that if there is a major situation or circumstance in your life you want to change, that either keeps repeating in a negative way, or is outside of your ability to believe, or even after trying numerous techniques has not worked, it is essential that you deal with any core beliefs you may have in order for the new reality to be created.

I am sharing all this information with you, so that you too, can experience the same transformative experiences that I have and begin to change your life to something better, full of all the things that you want in life.

I will now provide a summary of this chapter so it is all on one page for you to use.

CHAPTER 9.

Summary Of Exercises

(Carry out this exercise with pen and paper, it works more effectively)

Then ask yourself the questions below:-

What do I want to create in my life right now? *(This is the easy part because you will most likely be living the opposite of what it is you want to create, so just write down I want to create (answer) in my life).*

I wonder why I created this reality? *(What do you believe about this reality).*

What do you feel about the current reality?(Your Name)

(List down all the emotions you feel about the beliefs you hold about this situation)

What's all this about?(Your Name)

Read through your previous answers and then write down whatever comes into your mind and notice if there is a common theme.

What is the core belief preventing me from changing my current reality?*(now look through the list of negative core beliefs below and write down which ones relate to you from the answers you have written down).*

Negative Core Beliefs List

Feeling unsafe (basic needs not met food, water, warmth, clothing, abuse)
Feeling unloved (no hugs, facial contact, shouted at, screamed at)

Poverty (observing living in poverty, a mindset of not enough)

No sense of right or wrong (morals values not developed)

I am no good

I am unlovable

I am not enough

The world is unsafe (sometimes this can be created from being shielded from the world with the best possible intentions)

No good people in the world

I can't trust adults

I am undeserving

I deserve all the bad that is happening

I am worthless

I feel rejected by everyone and everything

I have no value

I am loathed by everyone

All the above examples are actual real stories of my life. I not only used to believe them, I used to talk about them constantly to everyone and moan about everything. Worse still the stories continued in my head nearly all day everyday.

It is really important to understand that the subconscious mind is not trying to harm you or hurt you. In fact it does not know the difference between right or wrong, good or bad. All the subconscious mind wants to do, is express in reality the beliefs that are active within you right now. If your current reality is good and happy and joyful, then you are expressing positive beliefs into your reality. If something is not working out, or is making you feel unhappy, you also have to recognise that this is a belief that your subconscious mind is expressing too. As you begin to look at life and ask the above questions you can begin to identify the beliefs active and be proactive in creating change in your life.

Now we can go onto the next section of the book "Change", where you can begin using powerful techniques to change your core beliefs right now.

CHANGE

CHAPTER 10.

Change

If you have faithfully followed the exercises up to this point you should now have identified a core belief(s) that is active within you and within your life. This is the section where we can really begin to change those core beliefs that have been holding you back.

What do you do now you have identified that belief, well to put it simply you just begin to change them. We do this through a process called reframing, this means that we convince the subconscious mind that the old belief / narrative that has been active within you no longer applies. It is an old story that was needed back then to support you in some way, but now it is no longer required and you want to create a new narrative a new belief system to support what you are wanting to create.

So the method I have used on myself and lots of the clients I have worked with is called 'Changing Beliefs Exercise', it is not the only method however it is an extremely effective method in helping reframe a belief system that is no longer serving a useful purpose. *(remember if you go to the website I have personally recorded this for anyone wishing to use this method.)*

This method is a two step process and is all about you accessing the current beliefs within you and changing them.

This method allows you to directly access your subconscious mind so that you can create a better relationship with yourself and let your subconscious mind know that the beliefs you currently have now need to change.

The reason this works is the subconscious mind cannot identify the difference between reality and imagination. If you think about eating a lemon now, or hearing the scraping on a blackboard, or even think about something you may be afraid of like a spider or mouse. Instantly you can find yourself feeling the sour taste in your mouth, or feeling the adrenalin rush because of the fear, or the uncomfortable feeling of the blackboard being scraped.

The reason for this is your thoughts are powerful and if you can convince your subconscious mind through imagination that something is happening. It will respond to the thought(s) that you have. Thoughts can even take pain away. I have proven this many times and it is in fact one of the many reasons I became a hypnotherapist so I could help my mother with pain relief.

Many times as a hypnotherapist I have dealt with clients who have had fears of flying, spiders, dentist, lifts. All these fears are just thoughts in your mind that your subconscious mind has made real for you. So all you are going to do with the technique I am about to share is let your subconscious mind believe that the current beliefs are no longer valid and that new beliefs can now be created. Most fears and anxieties are created not by the actual reality of a situation but by your own thoughts about the reality of the situation.

If you can convince your subconscious mind that something is true, it will make it true for you this will then create a different reality for you. It will create a reality where the new belief system is active.

When you read through the exercise commit it to memory, or record it and play it back to yourself, or if you prefer I have recorded a copy of this exercise on my website for you to use www. illuminateyourbrilliance.com

CHAPTER 11

Changing Beliefs
Exercise - Part 1

So what I want you to do right now is just close your eyes and just become aware of your breathing.

Just notice each breathe as it moves in and out of your body.

As you breathe in just take that deep breathe in filling your lungs with all that fresh air, and as you breathe out just allow that out breathe to flow out through your body, right down to the tips of your toes.

Breathing in and out, nothing to do, nothing to think about, nothing to even be aware of, this is your time, your time to be calm and comfortable, your time to be peaceful and rested.

Thoughts may flow into your mind and that is perfectly normal, it's perfectly natural, just allow them to flow in and out of your mind. Thoughts are like leaves on the trees with the branches just blowing in the wind, they are inconsequential now. You can just observe them from a place of peace, of tranquility, of serenity.

Each breathe out carrying you further taking you deeper, thoughts moving in and out of your awareness easily and effortlessly, as you just melt further and further into the chair, sinking deeper and deeper.

Calmly and comfortably and naturally, allowing yourself to be guided by my voice, to those deeper levels of relaxation. Where you can experience true peace and tranquility, your breathing slowing down to safe levels.

Every breathe out carrying you deeper into relaxation. All the systems of your body are beginning to slow down now, your heart rate and blood pressure all reducing down to safe and comfortable levels so that you can really enjoy this time of complete and total relaxation, a time of peace and calmness my voice guiding and inspiring you ever further.

All the sounds and noises that you may hear just allow you to sink further and further, deeper and deeper, my voice calming your mind and soothing your body. As you truly enjoy this experience, this space that is being created within you right now.

In a few moments I am going to count from 1 to 10 each number allowing you to drift to deeper levels of relaxation becoming calmer and so much more comfortable,

as I begin to count now

1…
2…
3…
Deeper and deeper further and further so much more comfortable now.
4…
5…

6...

Relaxing so much more so peaceful so calm

7...

8...

9...

Further and further now so calm, so peaceful, so rested.

10...

Completely and totally relaxed and still.

Your mind your thoughts are so clear now, nothing for you to do, nothing for you to think about, nothing for you to even be aware of right now other than being guided by my voice to a safe place, a place of peace, a safe place within you, a place where incredible change is possible for you right now.

In this place of calmness and peace, you have access to tremendous resources, you have access to insights and learnings, because you have access to your subconscious mind.

Just imagine what it's like now, to be with your subconscious mind, how would it be right now.

Maybe there are images or sounds or just a nice warm cosy feeling It might even be a knowing that your subconscious mind is their listening absorbing the words I am speaking right now. It does not matter what your experience is because your experience is unique and perfect and just right for you to create any and all changes that you want for your life right now.

So just know that deep within you right now your subconscious mind is eager to listen to my words because my words are with your approval and with your permission and my words can help you to create any change that you want for you life right now. My words can create any change in your beliefs right now this is because I am now in direct communication with your subconscious mind.

I want you to now begin to think about the last chapter where you began to identify the general beliefs and core beliefs from the past that have been holding you back. Maybe there is an element of uncertainty or maybe you identified one or two of those beliefs, it does not matter, there is no right or wrong in any of this.

You can just experience change in a way that is just perfect for you. Everyone has an element of limiting beliefs within them, a feeling of being unsafe in the world or unloved.

Just allow yourself to be really aware of those beliefs that have been holding you back.

It is really important to just allow this awareness to flow into your experience, maybe its a feeling of not deserving good things and experiences to happen for you or maybe a feeling of unworthiness, or a belief that bad things always happen to you. You may even believe that there is no one in the world you can trust or that the world is unsafe. Maybe there are negative beliefs about yourself that are no longer wanted.

Maybe you are not recognising your value to yourself and others, or the value of your skills of kindness, love and compassion. It could be a belief in the reality of poverty, just notice these are all limiting beliefs too.

Just allow all these negative beliefs that you hold just flow into your awareness right now, and as your subconscious mind is listening to my words you can become more aware of my words and the feelings that you have about these beliefs that are holding you back. Maybe you believed that you were creating a structure a safe space, or that these beliefs were protecting you from some imagined threat.

In this moment now your subconscious mind has an incredible ability to resolve these conflicts and outdated beliefs within you, that are creating the negative feelings and thoughts. All those old thought patterns are now being resolved. your subconscious mind as I speak these words has already started the process of dissolving these old outdated unwanted patterns of thoughts. These beliefs of you feeling unsafe, or the world feeling unsafe or of not trusting adults or feeling worthless or undeserving or not recognising your true value are not required anymore, maybe in the past they served a purpose, but now you are older and these beliefs serve no real purpose now and are no longer useful to you.

Now you are so much wiser and older and these beliefs that have held you back are no longer valid or needed or even wanted any longer.

It is time to give your subconscious mind permission to just release these beliefs, just make the decision right now deep within yourself, make the decision that these beliefs no longer serve you and your subconscious mind is carrying out all the necessary processing so that you are free from the past, so that all the old outdated beliefs are dissolved. So that all the conflicts and patterns of thoughts that have held you back up until now are resolved, so that you can now allow all those past negative beliefs to be released from your experience.

As you do this just become aware of that gentle release within you, that gentle feeling of calmness or warmth or maybe there are even goosebumps flowing throughout your body. Whatever you are experiencing is perfect for you. Know that your subconscious mind is now working for you in a really powerful way, letting go, releasing those outdated beliefs, recognising that they are of no value any longer. You can now move forward knowing that all those beliefs and thought patterns from the past can now remain there and you are free from their effect because they are all resolved now they have all been processed.

(30 seconds silence for subconscious to process)

Your subconscious mind is now ready for new seeds of thoughts new patterns of thoughts and beliefs, Your subconscious mind is now ready to embrace a new way of living life, a way where you can feel free, where you are supported encouraged and nurtured to live the life that you choose. Your subconscious mind is now creating beliefs that are helping you.

Just imagine now feeling safe and truly loved by your subconscious mind, imagine recognising your true intelligence and how special and unique you are, recognising all the talents and abilities that you possess, your intelligence, your kindness, your empathy, your warmth and capacity for love and so much more.

Know that your subconscious mind now truly recognises that you yes you truly deserve good things to flow into your life right now, because the world is safe the world is your playground now.

It is the playground from which your thoughts are played out upon and because you know this, the world suddenly feels full of opportunities. The world suddenly feels safe and you know the people within the world are there to support you and you can now trust in that new belief.

There is so much now that you have to offer because you recognise how worthy you are and how valued you are by everyone and how valued your skillset it.

The world is full of opportunities for you now, opportunities for you to create whatever it is that you choose for your life. You can feel free in the knowledge that everyone you meet is there to support your creation whatever that creation may be. You know that everyone and every situation you experience is there to inspire you too great things.

You have an inner intelligence, a uniqueness and special quality about you.

As you begin to notice how safe you truly are now, how nurtured you are, as your subconscious mind continues to feedback all of these incredible feelings throughout your body in waves, more and more you are becoming aware of your ability to create whatever it is you choose for your life. Beyond anything else know that you are a powerful creator, and more and more good feeling emotions begin to flow through you, guiding you to opportunities, guiding you towards a happy prosperous inspired life.

You have so much to offer, the value that is you, your subconscious mind feeds this to you, and you can now feel this within you, just feel right now your subconscious mind embedding these beliefs within you. Creating a sense of freedom a sense of opportunity a sense of abundance love and success. Just knowing now that every step every decision every choice you make from this moment forward is taking you to greater things, to greater opportunities to greater happiness to increased wellbeing.

Just know right now that you are enough, yes you are enough.

You are so worthy of these incredible feelings and emotions that are now flowing through you, because you know now the powerful creator that you are.

You can now trust yourself and your subconscious mind knowing that your subconscious mind will continue to bring forth inspiration for greater things to happen in your life to be happy and feel happy, to enjoy a life full of abundance and all of the resources that you want.

You are enough.

You are enough.

Take a minute now to really enjoy and fully experience the powerful creator that you truly are.

(Wait 1 minute break)

As you bring your awareness back to my voice, just know that you can move forward knowing that all those things from the past are resolved and you have stepped forward now to a fresh new life of freedom.

In a few moments I will awaken you and I will do this by counting up from 10 to 1 after 1 you can awaken refreshed and comfortable, calm and peaceful, knowing now that all those changes have happened for you and you can move forward to a life of freedom, love, abundance and happiness.

A newfound confidence and trust will be present in your thoughts a feeling that everything is just working out for you now, and as you move throughout the days you will be more present in the day.

You will begin to notice that everything truly is ok in your life and that everything is working out perfectly, you are free from the past, free to make new choices, free to live the life of your dreams, the life you want to live.

(Slight Pause)

I will now awaken you by counting from 10 to 1.

10…

9 ….

8 ….

Allowing all sounds and noises to return to there normal usual levels

7 …

6 …

5 …

Allowing all feelings of lightness and heaviness to fade away as you are now re-orientating yourself to the room you are in

4 …

3 …

2 …

1 … Eyes open and wide awake

Take your time to bring your awareness to the room and after a few minutes have something to eat or drink to ground you back into the present moment.

The Changing Belief recorded exercise part 1 can be found in this link,
www.illuminateyourbrilliance.com

Chapter 12.

Changing Beliefs Exercise - Part 2

It can take up to twenty one days for a new practised thought to become a habit. So for the next few weeks I would like you to consciously begin using the bubble of awareness technique discussed in section one awareness.

I want you to use it differently this time. Once you are inside the bubble I want the inner dialogue to be something like this:-

Example of dialogue

Life is good now, I have finally released those old outdated beliefs that were no longer serving me, I can finally relax in the knowledge that all those beliefs and old patterns of thoughts are now resolved within me.

I am finally free, I have finally let go, I can just enjoy life knowing that I have released those outdated beliefs, that no longer serve, they are old and outdated and I have finally resolved them with the help of my subconscious mind.

I am now creating new seeds of thoughts, new beliefs and new patterns of thoughts that are serving me and supporting me to live a full life, full of resources, abundance and all the things that I want. Life is good now. I feel so light now knowing that I am free from the hold of those past thoughts and beliefs. Free to move forward to a new life of good feeling emotions and experiences.

(It is important to use your words and not mine unless they resonate with you, the dialogue above is just an example).

For the next few days I want you to really build on the new emotional responses that will be created within you from the new inner dialogue. Really feel the certainty of this. Let yourself trust in your inner dialogue, and the changes that are happening right now.

Continue to have these conversations long after the 21 days, state all the issues from the past are resolved now, I can move forward to a better life, I have now released everything from my past relating to that old issue and am now moving forward, everything is ok now, everything is fine now and I can truly move forward to a new beginning where everything I want exists. I feel the complete and total trust that it is happening right now, I am completely and totally free.

You may even notice after a few days you will begin to truly feel changes as the new thoughts begins to create new beliefs within you. It is really important you do this exercise before going onto the next chapter and exercise, this is so the new beliefs are embedded within you.

The last two exercises are incredibly powerful at transforming negative core beliefs into something really positive. So please commit to them and commit to yourself. You deserve it.

CHAPTER 13.

Summary Of Exercises

Write down the core beliefs that are holding you back, read them through and remember them.

Now record, memorise or listen to the changing beliefs exercise on the website www. illuminateyourbrilliance.com to help you to change the core beliefs that are holding you back. You only need to listen to it once, but if you want to, you can listen to it as many times as you wish.

Now carry out the bubble of awareness technique but this time using the dialogue as described in the last chapter, ensuring the dialogue is conversational and unique to you by using your words.

CREATE

CHAPTER 14

How To Create what You Want

This is the most exciting section of the book. If you have followed the exercises up to now you will already have started to notice incredible changes in your life.

In order to create what you want, you first have to let your subconscious mind know what it is that you want. So in order to do this you have to ask.

The next technique is an adaptation of two techniques from one of my previous books "how to make the law of attraction work for you". In this book I describe the 'genie technique and the 'problem solving technique', for the purpose of this book I have adapted both techniques into one and have called it the "The Asking Technique'.

This technique is an effective way for you to let your subconscious mind know exactly what it is that you want to create in your life, and to begin to unleash the incredible creative power contained within you.

As I have mentioned previously your subconscious mind is tremendously powerful, especially in creating new, fresh and innovative ideas, and solutions to all sorts of challenges and problems that may be happening in your life.

Problems occur when you continue focusing on the problem, your brilliance then uses your creative power to keep you within the problem and situations. The reason for this, is the subconscious will only give you what you focus upon. If you are focused more on the problems and challenges than you are the solutions, then you just create more problems in your life.

When you begin to illuminate your brilliance by changing your negative beliefs and begin to focus on solutions and opportunities, you can then unleash your own brilliance and begin to create solutions, pathways and opportunities for you to create change in your life, increasing, or bringing greater;

abundance
happiness
Relationships
Health
Well being
Or anything else you want in your life.

The exercise to ask your subconscious mind is detailed in the next chapter.

CHAPTER 15.

The Asking Technique

This technique is simplicity itself, it is exactly what is says on the tin. You literally place yourself into a calm and peaceful place where you can communicate directly with your subconscious mind and ask for what you want. The only difference is in the way you ask.

So let's begin,

Close your eyes and just take several deep breaths, each time you breathe out just hear the word relax in your mind, continue to do this for several minutes.

It is important to take your time, and allow yourself to feel each breathe which will allow you to slip into a really calm and peaceful space.

After awhile you may find your thoughts becoming calmer and stiller, when this happens allow your breathe to return to normal and allow yourself to just experience the feeling of tranquility and calm. There is no right or wrong in any of this everyone will experience this in their own unique way.

It is important to take your time, there is no need to rush, everything is perfect right now, you are perfect and this moment is perfect.

I want you now to imagine that you are in a nice safe space, a field of flowers, a beach or just a space inside your own mind.

Take some time to allow yourself to see all the images and feel all the emotions in this safe place. I want you to engage all your senses into this experience.

Just imagine now that you are meeting with your subconscious mind, maybe you see images, or hear sounds, or just feel that you subconscious mind is there with you. You may just have a knowing that your subconscious mind is just listening beyond reach. Once you become aware of this just use the exact phrase below

Show me how I can create (whatever it is you want) in my life now?

Just remain with the question in your mind free from any expectation and just know that an answer will be made known to you either now immediately or in a few minutes or days later.

Now just create within you the feeling of the question being answered. Think about how it feels now, imagine a situation where you suddenly knew the answer to something it does not matter what it is, it could be a simple question someone has asked you and you suddenly knew the answer. A easy way to do this and it is my favourite is to imagine a train at the front of your head and as you ask the question show me how I can create (whatever it is you want) in my life now? Imagine the train travel to the back of your head and the subconscious mind is placing the answer in the train, then the train travels back to the front of your head and the answer is released into your awareness. You do not have to know the answer immediately but you do have to trust and believe the answer has been placed into your awareness now. Let this feeling / awareness grow powerfully within you, and remain with this awareness, this feeling for a few minutes, knowing and trusting the answer is there and is being made known to you now.

Now you can just count up from 1 to 5 and open your eyes and go about your day. This exercise is also on the website for your benefit should you wish to listen to the recoding I have done www.illuminateyourbrilliance.com

Now you have asked; your subconscious mind will provide an answer, a way forward, a solution.

The only thing to do now is to use your bubble of awareness with the dialogue below; If you have been practicing the bubble of awareness, you should find you can literally bring it into your awareness within seconds now so that you can carry out most of the exercises in this book whilst in that bubble.

As you move through your day continue to use the bubble of awareness stating, that everything is ok and nothing is wrong and everything is working out, the answers exist and are being made known to you in a really powerful way, there is nothing more for you to do right now, but listen to your own guidance, nothing more to do but listen to your own inspired thoughts, and allow the answer to just slip into your awareness, it is important to do this in a relaxed carefree way.

The answer to your question will come to you, and usually at an unexpected time when you are not really thinking about it. It may come at a time when you are distracted with something else, or after you awaken after sleep. You will receive an answer through inspiration, this is how the subconscious mind primarily communicates, through your feelings and thoughts. When you have an inspired thought this is your subconscious mind answering your question.

The reason we ask, Show me how I can create (whatever it is you want) in my life now?, is because when you ask to attract it, or manifest it, it implies that no action is taken by yourself and you can just sit back and wait for it to appear before you. This is not the case, it does not matter what philosophy is used, there will always be some form of action.

When you receive inspiration it will feel exciting and thrilling and fresh and new. All inspiration flows from the subconscious mind, and the inspiration you receive will always be a response to your question from the subconscious mind. When you receive inspired thoughts this is your creative self answering the question from the asking technique.

Your subconscious will also begin to nudge you in the right direction, you may experience thoughts as to what actions to take, or an idea may be generated in your mind and you will find that you will be placed in the right situations or circumstances, or meet up with the right people so that you are in the right place at the right time for you to notice and take any opportunities that are presented to you.

It is not important for you to know the whole plan or even how to get there. What is important is that you allow yourself to be guided by your own inspired thoughts.

Your emotions will be a good way of knowing if you are moving in the right direction, if your thoughts and actions feel good and you experience positive emotion, you are moving in the right direction. If however you are acting from a place of negative emotion you are moving in the wrong direction.

Everyone has experienced an inspired thought at some point once you receive the inspiration all that is required is for you to take action in relation to that inspired thought, we have all done this at some point in our lives and now this brings me nicely to the next chapter.

CHAPTER 16.

Inspired Action

What is inspired Action?

Let me explain every single thing that is created involves action. If you make a cup of tea you think about it before you actually get up and make it. If you mow the lawn, take the dog for a walk, make dinner for yourself, whatever it is you go through exactly the same process, detailed below:-

Feel an impulse *(eat, drink, walk, drive, shop, talk, socialise, buy etc etc.)*

A thought pops into your head how to do it.

Physical action is then taken.

The inspired thought is the first impulse that leads to the thought. Every single thing in life is created the same way it does not matter if it is the latest new gadget or a new business, or buying a lottery ticket, or even walking the dog there are always the same 3 steps.

There is one big difference though, if there are restrictive beliefs within you when you receive the inspiration the thoughts you have will be created from the negative belief, so all thoughts will then flow from that negative belief and you will act in a way that will create more things to support the negative belief. To put it more precisely you will act in a way that will create more of what you have.

Examples of inspired action when you have restrictive beliefs

Possible Belief -   I am unlovable, I am unworthy, I trust no one.

Impulse -   you go out with friends and feel an impulse a draw to a particular person.

Thought -	thoughts then come about what he / she would be like, whether they will like you or not.
Action -	action is taken you maybe speak or interact with this person, maybe even go into a relationship only to find that you are both incompatible or you are not treated in a good way.
Possible Belief -	I have no value, what I offer has not value.
Impulse -	feel inspired to set up a particular business.
Thought -	thoughts and ideas begin flow in about a how to create the business, what actions to take.
Action -	You start the business and it fails, or you work so hard you don't have time for anything else and you feel more trapped than you were before. Another aspect could be you doubt yourself and lack belief in what you do and make mistakes.

The examples above are just possible scenarios of how the process works. You will however recognise if an inspired thought will work out in a good way or bad way by the way you feel.

Your emotions will always guide you. If you have doubts or powerful emotions that tell you it is maybe not the best thing or the right thing, do not follow the impulse, as it is coming from a restrictive belief. This is where you will do the previous exercises to create a change in your beliefs.

Your emotions are literally guiding you all of the time informing you constantly whether you are moving in the right direction.

Remember my example of the public speaking I had the inspiration to do it and it felt wonderful at first, but once the idea had settled within me I started to get anxious and have a lot of doubts and all of this because my beliefs had got in the way, and needed to survive. Once I had changed the beliefs I was free to follow the inspired thought from a place of feeling really good.

I will now use the same two examples so that you can understand that the inspiration / impulse is always the same.

Remember the Impulse is the inspired thought.

Possible Belief -   I am lovable, I am worthy, I trust people around me

Impulse -   your out with friends and feel inspired to talk to a girl / man.

Thought -   thoughts flow into your mind I bet he or she is really nice, they look honest. I think they like me, and why not I am worth liking.

Action -   you talk to the person or they talk to you, maybe become friends fall in love.

Possible Belief -   I have value, what I offer is of great value, I am good at what I do.

Impulse -   You feel inspired to set up a particular business.

Thought -	thoughts flow in about how to create that particular business.
Action -	you start the business and you find things flowing, your in the right place at the right time, people come into your life who can help. Everything just seems to work out at the right time in the right way. There is no struggle, solutions flow on the back of any issues. You truly believe in yourself and the business you have established. Challenges may appear but solutions appear just as quickly.

This time you will be experiencing positive emotions that will guide you to do and say the right thing, for everything to just work out.

Inspired thoughts are just inspired thoughts they can take you to whatever you want to create. Your beliefs, thoughts and emotions will determine whether it will create more of the same or worse, or be positive and create what you want in life, abundance, happiness, love, success and more joy.

Just remember if you ask for what you want and you receive inspiration to act. Check in with your emotions just to find out if there are negative or positive beliefs guiding you.

The techniques are best used with the bubble of awareness. I cannot emphasise enough that the bubble of awareness is a way to switch your focus from what is currently being experienced in your reality, to something better because it simply brings your focus right into the present moment.

In our minds when a perfect moment is created we feel good, we feel joyful, we experience complete and pure bliss. In fact everything just feels right and perfect in the world. I have experienced this on many occasions in my life, usually when I am on some far flung beach enjoying the sunset with all the different shades of orange and yellow with the salty air blowing in my face and the warm sand beneath my feet, the turquoise waters lapping against the shore, in fact the entire experience just places me into a space of complete and total bliss and trust that everything is fine with the world and me and all is well.

When I am in these moments I am truly at one with myself and the environment around me and I truly do know that everything truly is ok and everything is just perfect. In these perfect moments life feels good, nothing is wrong, everything is just working out as it should. All sense of urgency just dissipates, allowing the experience to just flow within me in a completely perfect way. In these moments I just trust unconditionally that all is well, and that everything is complete and there is nothing more to do, and I can just enjoy the fruits of the moment. This is creating a perfect moment.

(Funnily enough this is the exact same emotional space that can create and bring whatever you want into your life).

There is only one reason that these perfect moments are not experienced more frequently within daily life, and the reason is your negative thinking about a particular situation, person, object, or even the absence of something in your life.

Thoughts continually give you a narrative about a situation that you choose to believe and as you believe those narratives an emotional response is then created within you. The emotional response from these narratives will guide you to make choices that will take you from the reality you want or to the reality you want.

Now you have received your inspiration and may even have begun taking steps to creating what you want, how do you build and keep the momentum?

You do this by creating perfect moments,

So how do you create a perfect moment?

As with most the exercises in this book using the bubble of awareness to create perfect moments is the most effective way, however this time I want you to do something different once you are surrounded in your bubble begin to imagine you are with a trusted friend or family member, then

Think about how it felt when you got what you wanted and you are telling someone how amazing you feel, as a result of getting what you want.

It could go something like this:-

You: I just got what I want it feels fantastic
Friend: thats brilliant.
You: it is I have waited so long and now I have it, I feel absolutely thrilled and energised and it just feels so great
Friend: I am really pleased for you it sounds exciting
You: It is this stuff really works you know it really does I just feel so happy right now.
Friend: Well you deserve it you are such a lucky person
You: Oh thank you so much, but its not luck you know, its all about belief

Continue to have conversations like this where you are telling your friend how amazing life is now that you have what you want. Keep doing this until you really feel the excitement, you may even feel goosebumps throughout your body if you do; this is great as you truly are in the creation state.

Just remember do not be specific, you are not wanting to talk about the new car, new business, new love or whatever it is that you want. All you want to do is create an emotional state, so make sure you are non specific about what it is you want, that's what is needed in order to create more of those perfect moments in your life.

It is quite difficult to explain, but it is like a feeling of trust a feeling of great its done now and it feels fantastic. All you really want to do is create the end feeling, the feeling that what you want is there now, that feeling of completion, of satisfaction, of ease, of joy. This is not imagining, this is creating a feeling.

Do this within your bubble of awareness as often as you can, the more you do it, the quicker the results will be, then;

I want you to look for evidence in life of all the things that are working out for you no matter how small they are, it could be a small act of kindness, a kind word or finding a penny in the street, or the sun shining in your garden today, it does not matter what it is anything in your life that can provide evidence that makes you feel good acknowledge that it is there to let you know, you are moving in the right direction and everything is working out for you.

As you do this in combination with the bubble of awareness and the dialogue above, even for just a few days you will begin to experience those perfect moments I wrote about earlier and as these become more frequent, you will begin to notice more opportunities will begin to show up in your life and your inspired actions will then create what it is you want for your life.

Thoughts do become things, someone imagined a tv with people in a box, they then took action and the tv was created. If someone has a dream or vision for a house, first there is the impulse then the thought, then the action is taken to make it happen. On a more basic level you feel thirsty, your mind creates images of what you would like to drink, you then take action to create this.

All creation requires action, however the type of action I am talking about is inspired action, not the action of restriction and effort, but the action that feels fresh and inspired.

Once you receive the inspired thoughts guiding you to the first steps to create what you want, follow and act upon them. You may not know them all at once, you may only be able to see the first step in front of you at a time but those steps will be shown and sometimes things may seem to go wrong, don't let it be an issue continue to use the bubble of awareness to create those perfect moments, and answers and solutions will flow as quickly as the problem or challenge that exists. Remember you never know where the destination is taking you and what may seem wrong now may be the best thing to happen in order for you to get what you want.

Chapter 17.

Summary of Exercises

Carry out The Asking Technique

Use the bubble of awareness technique in the way described earlier with the dialogue below until you receive an inspired answer.

As you move through your day continue to use the bubble of awareness stating, that everything is ok and nothing is wrong and everything is working out, the answers exist and are being made known to you in a really powerful way, there is nothing more for you to do right now, but listen to your own guidance, nothing more to do but listen to your own inspired thoughts, it is important to do this in a relaxed carefree way.

Once you receive the answer you then act on that inspiration, it does not matter what as long as you act in a way that is moving you towards your goal, you will naturally receive inspiration as to what steps to take, and be guided by your subconscious mind.

Now use the bubble of awareness again to create a perfect moment and continue to do this until what you want has been created in your life. *(Refer to chapter 16 for greater detail)*

Everyday look for evidence that everything is working out, it does not matter what it is as long as it feels good use it as evidence that what you want is being created right now.

(Remember creating a perfect moment is the perfect state to be in for creating what you want, and if something seems to go wrong, remember nothing is wrong and it's just a stepping stone to where you are going and it's all part of the process.)

At times things will seem to go wrong, or you will be faced with issues and challenges, remember you do not know where that wrong thing is taking you.

It could be that the wrong thing is the biggest stepping stone to getting what you want. So if something appears to go wrong just see it as a stepping stone to where you are going, and instantly begin to use your bubble of awareness to create those perfect moments. Some of the most wonderful things in my life have come from a perceived problems.

An example of which I was in a relationship, and I was abandoned, at the time I did not realise it was a bad relationship I was in, all I could see was I was abandoned and alone and I was devastated.

Fast forward 3 months later I met the love of my life and we are still together. Without that so called wrong thing I would never have met Darren. So do not see problems as things to be overcome, see them as stepping stones to getting what you want.

CHAPTER 18.

Karma, Destiny
and Free Will

This chapter may upset some people as it may go against your current beliefs. I do want to make it clear though that these are my personal findings and opinions from the spiritual experiences I have had in my life and from the results I have experienced from creating my own reality.

Let's start with karma, what is karma?

Well karma states that whatsoever you do to someone, will return back to you threefold, whether it be good, or whether it be bad.

In what I call now, my witchy days, this was a big premise, a given, a fact of life and everyone believed it to be true. Me being me though, I could not understand it, it made no sense and with my curious mind I could not take it on face value and wanted to understand why it would work this way.

Without realising it I had already asked my subconscious mind for an answer and this is now my understanding of karma.

If we create our entire awareness, we cannot possibly be affected by karma for perceived sins, that implies that we do not create our reality, and this was always my dilemma with karma.

My own personal truth now is that we experience repetitive patterns in relationships and work and money and home life and all sorts of things purely and simply because we have negative core beliefs active within us.

The subconscious mind wants so desperately to let us know these beliefs exist and need to be changed that situations keep repeating and each time they repeat they become worse and worse until we stand up and listen and say hey, this is telling me something about me. When you realise this and begin to change those beliefs it is no longer necessary for that belief to be repeated because you have changed it to something much more beneficial.

This can be for anything imagine some of the beliefs people have, it can make them victim to all sorts of situations and circumstances. I know from my own experience of life I have been a victim to many things and blamed karma. The truth however was a bit different I just could not face up to the fact that my own beliefs were creating these victim states, because this would mean I was was the only one responsible for creating my reality and I did not want to face this fact back then. Once I did accept this, things changed really quickly and in fact my own parents just say to me now you are just a lucky person, but the fact of the matter is I'm not lucky I just chose to create a different reality by changing negative beliefs that were active within me to more positive beneficial beliefs.

What about destiny and free will

I was not going to put this in, but the other day I had a really powerful dream, probably one of the most lucid moments of my life and woke up instantly knowing I had to put this in the book. I do however intend to do more books to cover this subject in greater depth, this is just a taste of what is to come.

I was curious about creation what is it?, how does it work?, how do we actually create?,

I went to bed and it was incredible really I gained so many insights from my subconscious mind and I felt this incredible urge to share so here goes.

I saw myself surrounded by bubbles of realities all centred around me and there were bridges to each and every reality, some were small bridges, others were miles and miles long. When I woke up I just knew what it all meant.

Imagine if you will that there is an infinite field and on this field are bubbles with every single possible reality you could possibly experience.

Everything from winning the lottery, to being a celebrity, from being poor to being a successful business person, to being in love, to being alone, any and I mean any possible reality is a bubble on this field connected by pathways or bridges. All of these potential realities could be called destiny as they dictate that everything is possible and every choice you could possibly make already exists as a bubble of reality, destiny.

Free will comes into effect because in the physical life you have now you cannot experience every potential choice, or reality that exists, so you use your free will to experience these bubbles of reality by the beliefs that you hold and the thoughts you think, and when you believe something powerfully enough you literally synch up with the new reality.

The bridges or pathways can be near or far and their distance to where you are is determined by how believable a potential reality is to you.

As an example you have a belief that you are hardworking and loyal to your company, you wake up in the morning and choose to

Eat your breakfast and leave to get to work on time, as soon as you do this,

Other realities exists where:-

You made a decision to have no breakfast
Or you made a decision to stay in bed
Or you made a decision to call in sick
Or you made a decision to get up late and eat breakfast on the go

There are many more scenarios I could mention, but hopefully you get the idea. Your beliefs will determine what choice you make and how far along the bridge of beliefs these potential realities are.

So in effect you have free will within infinite potentiality that already exists.

What this actually means is that everything you could ever want to experience or have in life already exists, and the only thing stopping you from having the experience of the new reality are the beliefs you hold.

Think about it now, you could experience any reality just by creating a new belief and this then allows you to travel along that bridge of belief to a new reality. My theory is the bridges represent how close you are to believing the potential reality or not believing the potential reality.

So if you believed that you would go to work tomorrow and experience the same things, because it is your belief, the bridge of belief would be close and it would be relatively easy for you to synch up with it.

If you wanted to synch up with a reality of you for instance winning the lottery or receiving a multi million pound idea, you may not believe that as easily so the bridge of belief to that reality is longer and this would mean you would have to work on changing your beliefs to get closer to that reality in order for you to synch up with it.

Taking this a step further drawing on my witchy background, this means that no future could truly be predicted, and all the clairvoyant or psychic is seeing are the current beliefs held within the person they are reading.

The psychic is only seeing the current beliefs active, because thought always precedes creation so in order for a psychic to know the future they have to be aware of the current beliefs and thoughts contained within the individual, which sounds more like telepathy.

Interesting stuff, however I do need to emphasise that these are my own personal beliefs. They are not important in relation to the exercises in this book and you do not have to believe any of this in order to get the techniques to work, but it is something that I personally believe and think about a lot. Even stranger is the fact I have an exercise in my other book called bridging beliefs.

Anyway that's enough of that and if you are interested in more stuff like this drop me an email, my details are on my website which are at the end of the book.

CHAPTER 19.

Final Words

So how do I conclude this book, what are my final words.

See the statements below.

Today is worse than yesterday because today I have had more things to stress and worry about in my life today. Tomorrow will be even worse because I had more time to think about all the worry and negativity from today, that will be created in my life tomorrow.

The above is exactly how most peoples thought processes are.

In order to create a new reality for yourself you have to break free from the cycle, you have to think different thoughts. Look at the statement below:-

Today is better than yesterday because today I have been living some of the good thoughts from yesterday. Tomorrow will be even better because I have had more time to think and feel good thoughts today, so more will be created tomorrow to let me think more good thoughts and feel more positive emotions.

You are a powerful creator!

You just have to choose if you want to create more of what you have, or create something completely new.

If you choose to stop creating by default and instead want to truly recognise your brilliance, then begin to be more selective about your thoughts, choose to change what is holding you back. Take back control of your life.

Only you can do this, but you can, I am living proof that this process works

You can do this, I have done this in my own life, and once I decided to take control of my beliefs and thoughts, my life began to change in incredible ways.

Everything you need to release the beliefs that are holding you back is contained in this book, but it takes a commitment to the exercises.

I have made it much easier by posting recordings of the main techniques on my website. There are no excuses, other than the excuses you create for yourself.

You deserve a better life filled with all the things that you want. Take that step, make that commitment to yourself and follow through with the instructions in this book, and please feel free to email me and let me know of your successes, I would love to hear from you.

So enjoy life, it is meant to be enjoyed, allow yourself

A life of freedom
A life of joy

A life of love
A life of Abundance
A life of success
A life of happiness
A life which you deserve

Much love, success and joy to you all

Mike

BIBLIOGRAPHY

England, Mike, How to make the law of attraction work for you, Authorhouse, 2009

England, Mike, Miracles happen with one good thought Createspace, 2011

Murphy Joseph Murphy Revised by Ian McMahon
The power of the subconscious mind
Pocketbooks, 200,2006

Genevieve Davis, Becoming Magic
Amazon 2014

Hicks Esther & Jerry,The Teachings of Abraham
Ask and it is given
Hay House UK 2005

Bach Richard, Illusions
Arrow Books 1998

Jane Roberts, A Seth Book, Seth speaks
Amber Allen Publishing 1998

RESOURCES

Further information can be found on my website and the recordings of some of the exercises in this book are recorded personally by me on the website below:-

www.illuminateyourbrilliance.com

I can be contacted by email on the website above.

Please post your successes on my instagram and Facebook pages, I love to hear of peoples success.

Search #illuminateyourbrilliance on Facebook, instagram and youtube.

www.ingramcontent.com/pod-product-compliance
Lightning Source LLC
Chambersburg PA
CBHW060542160726
47991CB00001B/418